CONGRESS IN THE SEVENTIES

STEPHEN K. BAILEY

Maxwell Professor of Political Science, Syracuse University

ST. MARTIN'S PRESS • NEW YORK

For Morrie—

who shares, and who hopes to preserve and extend, the blessings of a free society

Library of Congress Catalog Card Number: 70-102721
Designed by Jeanette Young
Printed in the United States of America.

Contents

Preface

This book is part analysis, part normative judgment, part prophecy. Analytically, it deals with the place of the United States Congress in the American constitutional and political scheme and with the organization and procedures that reflect the peculiar power base of our national legislature in the early 1970's. The book's normative judgments relate to the collective performance of Congress and to standards (or lack of them) governing the behavior of individual members. As prophecy, the book attempts to identify some of the secular forces that appear to be determining the American destiny and the role of Congress in shaping that destiny between now and 1980.

Speculation of this kind is hazardous. The earlier version of this book, published in January 1966 under the title *The New Congress*, identified correctly many aspects of what was then the future. But, in retrospect, it underplayed the impact of the Vietnam war upon both domestic and international political developments, and it failed to note the limitations that intractable economic and fiscal forces necessarily impose upon political discretion—at home and abroad.

Its basic theme, however, was not significantly overstated: "that basic political, economic, and sociological changes in the American society, and in the world at large, have finally forced a series of adjustments in the structure and role of Congress so profound as to merit the term 'revolution.'" Certainly, compared with congressional behavior of the 1950's, the "New Congress" of the 1960's was far more sensitive to the claims of the American Blacks and to the needs of urban populations generally. If Black militancy, crime in the streets, student unrest, war, and inflation have slowed the desire for, and possibility of, a repetition of reform cornucopias like those the 89th Congress spilled forth, pressures for the full funding of old programs and the creation of new ones have not disappeared. And in certain areas like welfare legislation, tax reform, revenue-sharing with state and local governments, and defense policy, what would have seemed in the 1960's totally improbable changes are already occurring in the Congress—and with bipartisan support.

Furthermore, the decline of southern power, identified in *The New Congress* a half-decade ago, goes inexorably on. As the decade of the 1970's begins, of the ten Democratic senators with the greatest seniority, nine come from south of the Mason-Dixon line. Most of these are men in their seventies or older. Of the ten ranking next in seniority (the heirs apparent of those ancient Democrats about to depart the scene) only two come from the American South.

With the disappearance of the inordinate power of southern conservatism the real question arises: Will a new, nationally based, petty-bourgeois, anti-tax, anti-Black conservatism become the dominating force in the Congress in the 1970's? There are many who predict just such a development.

The author doubts the likelihood of such an outcome. To the contrary, his prediction is that viable politics in the 1970's will be based upon awkward but increasingly promising coalitions between racially ghettoed Blacks and economically ghettoed whites—both in cities and in suburbs. Robbing second-generation, working-class or lower-middle-class, Polish-American "Peters" to pay the welfare costs of Black-American "Pauls" has no political future. The lower two-thirds of the American population (in terms of income) will increasingly unite against those individuals and groups in the upper third who for generations have manipulated the instruments of American government and politics to gain special favors, special services, special subsidies, and special tax concessions for themselves. Lower-and middle-class families together will increasingly demand the kinds of health services, education services, transportation services, housing opportunities, and recreational facilities that over the years have been lavishly and inequitably subsidized with public funds for the benefit of a relatively small minority of the American population. In this national struggle for equitable sacrifice and services, the manifest and latent bigotry in America will become increasingly muted. Marriages of convenience across racial-political lines will at times be stormy, but the marriages will last and become less sour as additional commonalities of interest are discovered.

And, as suburbs become increasingly brindled with middle-class

Black families escaping the pathologies of central cities, the politics of class will increasingly supersede the politics of group identity in our national life. This process will be hastened as Blacks in increasing numbers graduate from colleges and professional schools, and as a colorblind generation of younger whites assumes its place in the world of work and affairs.

The New Congress in the 1970's will increasingly respond to these new claims and coalitions. Pragmatic Nixon Republicans and urban-oriented Democrats will increasingly join hands—replacing the rurally based Southern Democrat—midwestern Republican alliances of the past.

In foreign affairs, Congress will attempt to augment its control over the Presidential prerogative in order to preclude a repetition of the Vietnam escalations of the mid-1960's. But foreign affairs are dynamic and unpredictable. Predictions of a return to the isolationism of the 1920's and 1930's seem to the author naive and immoral. The author's crystal ball foreshadows only a substantial drawing back from unilateral peace-keeping activities in distant jungles. America's influence abroad—military, diplomatic, and economic—will be made manifest increasingly through international and multilateral channels. Both Congress and the President will assume initiatives in pushing the nation in this direction. It is the only way to avoid both local Vietnams and global holocausts. The logic of any meaningful détentes with the Soviet Union and of any viable probes through the Bamboo curtain rests on international and multilateral action.

The basic function of Congress has always been, and will continue to be, law-making. Throughout human history, even under most despots, governmental powers have been shared, with a council being given the power to "legitimate norms." The other powers of Congress—to appropriate, to investigate, to mediate, to alleviate, and to repudiate—are all based on its power to legislate. Through these powers Congress has played a leading role in the drama of American history. In the past two generations alone Congress has been forced to adjust to cataclysmic changes—international and domestic, social and scientific, political and economic. It is true that Congress's adjustments to some of these changes have been slow, and that it has sometimes failed to take a responsive role. It is also true that parochialisms and anachronisms remain, but these have been substantially modified. The balance has swung irrevocably toward the cosmopolitan, rather than the parochial; toward the centripetal pull of presidential and party influence, rather than the centrifugal force of congressional committees.

If there is still a way to go in finding a fully appropriate congressional role in foreign affairs and in administrative surveillance generally; in correcting the lumpiness of advantage of selected group interests and "sub-governments"; in rationalizing the scatteration and overlapping of committee jurisdictions; in modernizing certain archaic procedures and practices, like those involving seniority; in helping centripetal forces in Congress to counteract traditionally dominant centrifugal forces; the fact remains that recent and prospective changes in our national legislature merit the term "revolution," and the revolutionary process continues. The New Congress of the 1970's will be more truly representative of the nation's population, more infused with the notion of equal opportunities and equitable services for all Americans, less permissive of presidential and military whim in foreign affairs, and more thoroughly committed to international solutions to international problems than the Congress of either the 1950's or 1960's. And its traditional structure and procedures will increasingly adjust to meet these new claims and pressures.

I rest my case upon direct observation, reflection, and interviews, and upon a wealth of first-rate scholarship that has appeared in recent years on the subject of Congress and the American legislative process generally. Those of us for whom the earlier generation of scholarship was confined very largely to intuitive and narrative approaches to reality have seen our insights refined, qualified, quantified, corrected, and sometimes verified by new tools of social science analysis. I have attempted to reflect my indebtedness in footnotes and in a selected bibliography at the end of the book.

Roughly the chapters that follow fall under three rubrics: the first three chapters deal with the *environment* of the "New Congress"; Chapters IV, VI, and VII with the *system;* Chapter VIII with the *norms.*

Special thanks are due for a variety of services to the following people: James MacGregor Burns, Richard Fenno, Bertram Gross, Earl Latham, Nicholas Masters, H. Douglas Price; and to Violeta Baluyut, Robert Blanchard, Marian Borst, Betty Gere, Priscilla Gortner; and especially to my assistant Joel Berke. The patience, judgment, and research assistance of my wife are reflected on every page. All errors in fact and interpretation are my responsibility alone.

STEPHEN K. BAILEY

Syracuse, New York
November, 1969

Chapter I

THE ELECTORATE

Elections are at the heart of representative government. So pervasive is the idea today of government by and with the consent of the governed that even modern dictatorships provide for at least the shadow of electoral legitimacy—insuring, of course, that electoral choices are controlled.

In America, the notion of elections as the key to popular control of legislators and officials goes back a long way. Even before our existence as a nation, the American colonists developed the custom of frequent elections for numerous offices, including legislative positions. After independence, but before the Federal Constitutional Convention, most of the new state constitutions provided for annual election of legislators. In justifying the clauses relating to the elections of representatives in Article I of the Constitution, the authors of the Federalist Papers wrote,

> . . . it is essential to liberty that [the House of Representatives] should have an immediate dependence on and an intimate sympathy with the people. Frequent elections are unquestionably the only policy by which this dependence and sympathy can be effectively secured.[1]

A two-year term for members of the House, a six-year term for members of the Senate, and a four-year term for the President were fundamental to the Founding Fathers' grand design of representative government. Staggered terms for the President and the two houses of Congress constituted an electoral device for promoting and insuring the doctrine of the separation of powers. If the nonjudicial branches of the federal government had been subject to identical and coincidental terms, America would have emerged as a parliamentary system in which executive and legislative authority had been effectively merged.

Localism and Representational Equality

American national legislators must not only be elected in order to hold legitimate power, they must be elected *locally.* This, of course, has always been true in the Senate; where, constitutionally, representation is by state. For most of American history this has also been true in the House of Representatives. Almost consistently since 1842, by law or custom, states having more than one representative have established congressional districts as the geographic base for representation in the House. It is true that under the Permanent Apportionment Act of 1929, states entitled (after decennial census) to an additional number of representatives may set them up "at-large" rather than rearranging existing district lines. But this is in fact exceptional. In 1968 only 7 out of 435 representatives were elected "at-large," and all of these came from states entitled to only one representative. Four hundred and twenty-eight House members, therefore, represented subunits of the several states called congressional districts.

In 1964 the United States Supreme Court, in one of the most important decisions in its history, declared that "one man's vote in a congressional election is to be worth as much as another's."[2] What would seem to have been the obvious intent of the Founding Fathers had over the years been warped out of shape by the unwillingness of rurally dominated state legislatures to redraw congressional district lines to take account of the urban drifts of the American population. In consequence, until the Supreme Court's decision in *Wesberry v. Sanders,* some congressional districts had four or five times the population of other congressional districts. The long-range effect of the court's decision will be to move power in the House away from rural and provincial and towards cosmopolitan and metropolitan viewpoints and interests. The shift has already begun. Virtually every state in the Union (excepting only those states with a single representative) underwent redistricting during the 1960's. The process will have to start all over again in the 1970's, not only because of demographic shifts reflected in the 1970 census, but because the Supreme Court, in April 1969, indicated its disapproval of many of the reapportionments of the 1960's. In *Kirkpatrick v. Preisler* and *Wells v. Rockefeller* the Court held that even a population variance from precise mathematical equality of 3.1 percent between or among congressional districts was unconstitutional—at least without justification that such a variance from "one man–one vote" was technically unavoidable. This decision called into question districts in 44 states which had undergone reapportionment in the 1960's. The *Wesberry, Kirkpatrick,* and *Wells* cases represent a basic long-range shift in political power in the United States. Their consequence is to promote redistricting after each decennial census in the future. Power will follow population or will be challenged in the courts. The legislative hold of sparsely settled rural populations over urban and suburban communities, in which the bulk of the nation's population lives, is mostly a thing of the past—although the practice of seniority and the gerrymandering of district lines* can keep parts of the anachronism alive for some years to come.

The tradition of localism in our national legislature is based not only upon the requirement that elections be held locally—by states and by congressional districts—but upon the constitutional provision that candidates for election be residents of the states (and by implication and practice, of the districts) from which they are elected. The custom of local residency for legislative representatives actually began in colonial times. This is in contradistinction to Great Britain, where faithful party members, no matter where they live, can be assigned by the party leadership to represent a "safe" district (i.e., a district which is overwhelmingly one party) anywhere in the country. The local residence requirement in the United States heightens a legislator's loyalty to his locality, and at least until recently has made the centripetal pull of the national party or of the Presidency at best uneven and complicated. The long-range effect of the redistricting cases, and of the Civil Rights Act of 1965, which opened the gates for massive Black registrations in the South, will be to make the constituencies of the overwhelming majority of congressional districts across the land socially and economically variegated. This increased pluralism will inevitably move House constituencies in the direction of becoming microcosms of senatorial and of presidential constituencies: metropolitan rather than rural, complex rather than simple, changing rather than stable. As the three constituencies increase their resemblance, there is reason to expect greater policy coherence across legislative and legislative–executive lines.

*The court was silent about the practice of gerrymandering—the drawing of congressional district lines in odd shapes designed to favor a particular political party. It is doubtful if the abuses of gerrymandering will ever be totally eradicated, although the worst offenses could be curbed by congressional action along the lines of a bill introduced by Congressman Emanuel Celler (HR 970, 89th Cong., 1st Sess., 1965). The Celler bill would mandate that districts "be composed of contiguous territory, in as compact a form as practicable."

Nominations

Before a candidate can be elected to Congress, he must, of course, be nominated. In most states, nomination comes about through a direct primary election. In a few states the party convention system is still used. In heavily one-party states or districts, nomination by direct primary is tantamount to election, since the victor in the primary will face little or no opposition in the general election.

Making nominations is pre-eminently the business of local political parties. Where parties are strong and highly competitive they tend to devote substantial time and energy to identifying and cultivating attractive candidates. Where parties are either weak or noncompetitive, the nominating process can be a shambles and/or can result in the nomination of a nonentity. For example, in some southern states, where the Democratic party is nominally strong, but organizationally weak and noncompetitive, anyone with a few kinfolk and courthouse friends can file for the primary. Even if a second or run-off primary is called for (as it is in most one-party states), the victor may have few qualifications for the job of representing his own district, let alone the national interest. A number of northern congressional districts in large one-party and machine-dominated urban areas have witnessed a succession of mediocrities in their nominations for representative. Without effective competition from a strong opposition party in their areas, many urban party leaders have used their power over House nominations to reward party hacks who have viewed congressional service as a patronage assignment and as something not to be taken too seriously.

But in at least two-thirds of the states and in at least half of the congressional districts in the United States, nominations for senators and representatives are considered of sufficient importance to warrant the careful and extended attention of party leaders. In such areas, the direct primary election is viewed as something to be influenced wherever possible by prior decisions of a caucus of political leaders or through a primary convention. In these terms, the chief business of the party is to select an attractive and loyal candidate, to discourage other strong candidates from challenging its candidate in the primary, and to insure that the party faithful come out to vote for the endorsed candidate in the primary election. Experience has shown that the general public is reasonably apathetic about primaries, in contrast to general elections. A small group of party regulars, therefore, can usually dominate the results of a primary election, even though, as V.O. Key reminded us, the existence of primaries does extend democratic influences over political machines.

The lesson of all this is that if one wants to run for the United States Senate or House of Representatives, he is prudent to cultivate the acquaintance of those local politicians whose major claim to power is their influence over nominations. The President and the national party organizations normally stay aloof from the nominating process.

What is of even greater value than local party support is to be already a United States senator or representative, for few incumbents are denied renomination. The reasons are obvious. Not only would a party's denial of the right of an incumbent to succeed himself look like an admission of his failure to achieve a commendable record; the incumbent has a vast number of built-in advantages as a candidate. He is known. He has had an opportunity to build support through a variety of services to individual constituents. He keeps tuned to the interests of important groups in his constituency. His time in office has given him valuable experience in legislative matters and seniority on the ladder of legislative power. So powerful are these advantages that when added to the number of one-party districts in the United States, they have produced an extraordinarily stable membership in the past fifty years, especially in the House of Representatives. H. Douglas Price estimates that "three-quarters of all House districts are relatively 'safe' year after year," leading to what he calls the "professionalization of the House career."[3]

The Senate, representing multi-interest states, is more subject to close competition, and consequently turnover, than the House. Even here, however, the continuity in office is substantial. The average length of service in the Senate is nearly ten years, and a quarter of the Senate has served for fifteen years or longer.

For the nonincumbent, prior political service in another elective office is highly desirable: for an aspirant to the Senate, prior service as a representative or a Governor; for an aspirant to the House, prior service in the state legislature or in a county or local office. Experience in winning votes and in handling public issues in the rough-and-tumble of debate and decision-making is a valuable asset for those who aspire to the national legislature.

A final desideratum, especially for the Senate, is financial independence. As we shall see, the costs of campaigning are substantial. A potential candidate who can throw some of his own private resources into the contest has a definite edge in the struggle for nomination and election over his less affluent competitors.

The Campaign

Once they have successfully garnered sufficient votes for nomination, most candidates face the arduous task of campaigning for election. One must use the word "most" because for some senators and representatives, hard campaigning during the weeks immediately prior to a general election is unnecessary. This is especially true of those who come from a "safe" state or district and who have already been, in effect, elected in the primary.

To most senators, to many representatives, and to all challengers of incumbents, however, intensive campaigning for election is an absolute necessity. No two campaigns are, of course, identical. It is even difficult to work out a typology of campaigns. The variables are extensive. The nature of campaign organization and strategy is affected by the answers to such questions as these:

—is the campaign in an "off year" (in a year when there is no presidential election)?
—is the candidate an incumbent?
—to what party does the candidate belong?
—if the campaign is conducted during a presidential year and the incumbent President is running for re-election, is the legislative candidate of the President's party; if not, is he in sympathy with the views and record of his presidential standard bearer?
—is the opponent relatively well known or unknown?
—is the state and local party well organized?
—is the press generally friendly or unfriendly?
—is the state or district large or small in geography? in population?
—are there crucial and reasonably cohesive interests in the electorate whose bloc voting may determine the outcome of the election (e.g., Blacks, workers, farmers, defense industries, oil interests, etc.)?

The answers to these and other questions will help to determine how a campaign is organized and conducted.

But in spite of these variations, certain needs, fears, and activities mark almost all campaigns for the Congress.

Campaign Financing

By all odds the most pervasive reality is the need for money—for campaign funds. Money must be found to pay workers, to rent offices and hire halls, to buy advertising services and public opinion polls, to purchase time on television and radio, to cover the costs of telephone and travel, to manufacture and distribute campaign buttons and campaign literature. In a populous state, the costs of a Senate campaign may run to a million dollars or more for each candidate. Even in a small congressional district, $25,000 to $50,000 may be needed by each candidate to finance an eight-weeks' campaign. Incumbent legislators who have franking privileges (the right to mail at the taxpayer's expense) and who can use their Washington and hometown offices for a variety of constituent services and public relations activities, have, of course, a built-in advantage. But even so, the search for additional campaign funds is a constant necessity.

Where does the money come from? The answer to this question may determine in part the answer to another question: once elected whom does a congressman* effectively represent? For if the funds for a particular candidate's campaign come substantially from one source, or one type of source, there is always the danger that "he who pays the piper calls the tune." The distortions in representation caused by "fat cats" may in fact be no greater than distortions caused by deference to crucial minority blocs whose votes can swing elections in evenly matched contests. But control or substantial influence over a candidate's campaign funds does cause a peculiar lumpiness of advantage in our representative system. Perhaps no issue creates more crises in conscience than how to find sufficient campaign money without sacrificing independence of judgment and equality of access once elected.

Fortunately, although the financial problem is becoming more difficult, the ethical problem is becoming somewhat easier. In one sense, the very size of the campaign budget is a help. The more expensive the campaign, the less likely that any one source can exercise a commanding impact upon the total enterprise. No one individual or interest, for example, could possibly "buy" a President. If no other factors were at work (and, of course, they are), the very magnitude of the budget of a presidential campaign would preclude the dominant influence of any single giver. To a lesser extent, the same principle holds true at the level of senatorial and congressional campaigns. Increasingly in recent years party organizations and candidates have turned to fund-raising dinners (anywhere from $25 to $1,000 a plate), featuring nationally known political figures as speakers. A thousand dollars is a lot for a single dinner, but if five hundred people each pay that amount to banquet with the President and to shake his hand, the possible influence of any one contributor on the party or candidate is insignificant. And if the half million dollars collected is then divided between the national committee (whose special concern is the presidential election) and the party campaign committees in the Senate and the House (whose business it is to offer financial and other campaign services to party candidates for the Congress), the linkage between donor and recipient is diffused.

This is not to suggest that in some congressional districts and in some senatorial races special interest money is unimportant. Labor unions, manufacturing and extractive industries, medical associations, commercial organizations, and a variety of affluent individuals and other interests may provide such a critical mass of financial support to particular candidates or party organizations as to threaten their independence and impartiality. And national interest groups may invest

---

*Unless otherwise clarified by context, "congressman" is used throughout to refer to members of both the Senate and the House of Representatives.

in a score of campaigns in a dozen different states and districts in order to maximize their impact in the Congress.

The most critical financial problems come at the level of the House of Representatives. Congressmen must campaign every two years. By and large, the formal structure of political parties by-passes the congressional district. The Democratic National Committee and the Republican National Committee collect and disperse money primarily for presidential elections. The state central committees of the two parties have their eyes particularly on gubernatorial and senatorial elections. County and city organizations are especially concerned with raising money for local candidates: mayors, commissioners, judges, etc. More than one congressional candidate has appealed in vain to these several levels of party organization for financial help. If he then turns to special interests inside or outside of his district for support, it is in no small part because his party has let him down.

Fortunately, recent trends are in the direction of greater interest of the national committees, the congressional campaign committees, and state and local committees in the fate of congressional races.

In 1965, for example, after the stunning Democratic victory in November 1964, the Democratic National Committee, in order to solidify the Democratic gains in the Congress, arranged a whole series of secret meetings with high-ranking administration officials "to speed the flow of federal funds and projects" into the home districts of freshman representatives. The Committee also hired publicists to write press releases and radio programs for congressmen; it made electronic equipment available for processing the mailing of congressional newsletters to constituents; it sent field men to many freshmen districts to organize "coalition support groups"; it sent speakers into districts and helped arrange speaking invitations for representatives.[4]

Although the Republican National Committee was less frenetic in its attempts to help Republican congressmen elected along with Mr. Nixon in 1968, 6,500 patronage jobs were open to the new administration and many of these have been used to please or placate particular congressmen. The hard-nosed game of "spoils" goes on regardless of party. The ideal piece of patronage is one that simultaneously serves the interest of the President, the party, and important congressional interests. This felicity is hard to attain, but it is increasingly being strived for.

As decisions in Washington affect states and localities with increasing force and frequency, and as congressional behavior increasingly affects the political destiny of Presidents and nations, the role of the individual congressmen becomes important—not just to friends and neighbors back home, but to everyone of importance in the national political system. Money follows recognition of value. Although it is doubtful that the national and state committees, or the congressional campaign committees, will soon dislodge local finance committes and interest groups as major sources of funds for congressional races, it is likely that the percentage of campaign revenue from party organizations will expand substantially in the coming years. This is a natural concomitant to the steady nationalization of American politics that has marked the past thirty years in American history.

As we shall note in the final chapter of this book, one other aspect of congressional campaign funds which deserves special consideration is the unreality of existing laws governing their solicitation, donation, and spending. Both the spirit and the letter of these laws are so frequently broken by our law-makers as to create widespread cynicism among politicians and within the general public.

The Advantages of the Incumbent

For the incumbent legislator, especially for members of the House, campaigning is an unending activity. The facilities and perquisites at his disposal for conducting a continuous campaign are so substantial that many congressmen "believe that, aside from isolated instances where an overriding issue is present, there is little excuse for defeat."[5]

Consider some of the incumbent's resources. First, there is the mail. Most congressmen receive hundreds of letters a week. Many senators receive hundreds of letters a day. These letters are answered at the taxpayer's expense under the franking privilege. Each answer—a favor granted, a problem successfully referred, a sympathetic note, a policy stand tactfully explained—is an opportunity to win a friend back home. "As one representative was told by his father, who had preceded him in the House, 'Son, I have three pieces of advice for you if you want to stay in Congress. One, use the frank. Two, use the frank. Three, use the frank.' "[6] Most congressmen and senators have their staffs prepare a weekly or monthly newsletter, which is sent under the franking privilege to a wide mailing list of important constituents. Such newsletters bring to the attention of constituents the activities of their national legislators, special grants or contracts assigned under federal law to the particular congressional district or state, news about hometown visitors to Washington, and other information designed to reassure constituents that their congressman is alive and on the job.

Second, congressmen are notables, at least locally. They are asked by scores of groups to appear for speeches or simply to grace a platform on a special occasion—a holiday parade, a high school commencement, the dedication of a new park. These events rarely have overt political meanings or leanings, but they provide golden opportunities for incumbents to exploit political advantages. As one congressman relates:

> Personally, I will speak on any subject. I am not non-partisan, but I talk on everything whether it deals with politics or not. Gener-

ally, I speak at non-political meetings. I read 48 weekly newspapers and clip every one of them myself. Whenever there is a particularly interesting item about anyone, that person gets a note from me. We also keep a complete list of the change of officers in every organization in our district. Then when I am going into a town I know exactly who I should like to have at the meeting. I learned early that you had to make your way with Democrats as well as Republicans. And you cannot let the matter of elections go until the last minute. I budget 17 trips home each session and somehow I have never managed to go less than 21 times.[7]

Third, facilities exist in the congressional office buildings to have radio and television clips made at cost. Except during the final weeks just before election, these may be broadcast in home areas as a public service without cost to the congressman.

Fourth, congressional offices prepare a stream of handouts to the Washington press corps, and they send news and feature items to dailies and weeklies back home. In many cases, these press releases are ignored by the press, or are chopped to two inches and buried in a back page. But even so, their cumulative effect on the public cannot be ignored.

Besides these broadside campaign devices, the incumbent congressman can and does perform a wide variety of services for individual constituents. Estimates range all the way from 50 to 90 percent of a congressman's time spent on constituent errands. Many of these services involve the congressman in an intermediary role between the constituent and executive departments and agencies: a veteran's pension check is late; a rumor has started that a local defense plant will be closed down; an internal revenue inspector has been arbitrary or officious; does the new Medicare Bill apply to noncitizens? The questions and problems are endless and infinitely varied. Much of the staff time in the offices of both senators and representatives is spent "bird-dogging" such issues. In addition, many requests come in that have little or no relation to the bureaucracy: "Can you get me seats to the Army-Navy game?" "I'm coming to Washington with my family over Easter vacation. Please get us hotel rooms." "I want to be a judge when I grow up. Can you get me a personal autograph of Chief Justice Burger?" "I am 13. Someday I should like to be an astronaut. Can you send me a signed picture of Neil Armstrong on the moon?" And, of course, there are a number of requests for jobs—especially as in the case of 1969 (or 1961) when a new administration and party has taken over the executive branch of the federal government.

Each of these requests presents an opportunity for the congressman to win the intense support of the person or interest helped. A service well rendered can result in a favorable word-of-mouth campaign back home which can be of significant political value.

Perhaps the final advantage of the incumbent is his inherent ability to stress the positive in the heat of an electoral campaign. Most people shun controversy. They dislike the snarling accusers and the prophets of disaster. The incumbent can point with pride to his own and to his party's record. He can speak as a magnanimous statesman and a friend of all the people. He can bask in the light of his experience.

The poor challenger must attack. He must view with alarm, point with fear. If he cannot worry his constituents with his opponent's record, what justification is there for throwing the rascal out? In spite of Mr. Nixon's victory in 1968, a strongly Democratic majority continued in the Senate and House, so difficult is it to displace an incumbent.

Campaign Strategy and Tactics

No matter how carefully an incumbent has wooed his electorate during his term of office, he shares with his challenger the stress and strain of pre-election campaigning. One astute observer of the political scene once commented that all political campaigns in the United States are governed by "an iron law of chaos." In one sense this is true. For most campaigns are conducted by too many chiefs and too few Indians, and the course of political events is unpredictable and often perverse. The most carefully considered strategy for a congressional contest may be negated by events twelve thousand miles away, by nationwide drifts in public sentiment, by sudden disclosures, by sudden deaths.

And yet within these limits and the limits of variables noted earlier, the fundamentals of campaign strategy are fairly constant. The task is to call attention to the record and the abilities of the candidate, to expose the inadequacies of the opposition, and to develop personal images and policy issues that will attract the support of a majority of citizens in the state or district.

Campaign headquarters must be established. Posters and literature must be prepared and distributed. Registration drives and door-to-door or telephone canvasses must often be undertaken. Radio and television time and newspaper advertising space must be reserved. Itineraries and campaign themes must be plotted. Speeches must be drafted. Often opinion polls are felt to be necessary in order to gauge the public's views of candidates and issues. An inordinate amount of time must often be taken in clearing and coordinating with other candidates and with various levels of party activity. Appropriate audiences and interest-group contacts must be arranged. Hands must be shaken; babies must be kissed. For some, but not many, congressional candidates, the exhilaration exceeds the exhaustion. The only real advantage of the challenger is that he may be able to work full time at campaigning while the incumbent must often divide his time between Washington and his home state or district in the crucial final weeks before election. But by the final week in October, both candidates are equally fatigued. Few occupations call for greater spurts of latent effort than politics. The expenditure of physical, emotional, and intellectual energy during the last laps of a hard-fought campaign is difficult to convey in words.

The Election

All of these efforts and activities have, of course, one final objective: victory at the polls. The high drama of election night is shared by the general public. The candidates and their immediate families, friends, and campaign workers follow the mounting returns with a particular excitement and concern. Dozens of persons have careers at stake in each contest: the candidate himself, his staff, those whose lives will be affected by patronage appointments, and others.

Once the election is over, it is rarely clear, beyond the simple categories of partisan victory and defeat, what the voters had in mind. In one sense, an election settles everything and settles nothing. It indicates who is to hold power, but it rarely suggests except in the most general way what the victor is to do with his power, or what precisely the voters held against the loser. Party preferences are a major clue to the meaning of electoral choice, but even here the story is not simple. A Republican victory in Alabama does not carry with it the same set of influences and attitudes as a Republican victory in New York City or Vermont. Senators James Eastland (Mississippi), Alan Bible (Nevada), and Edward Kennedy (Massachusetts), are all Democrats. But if their voting records and public pronouncements on issues are reflective in any way of opinions in their respective states, the only conclusion is that the Democratic party is a highly versatile and permissive political instrument. Even with these complications, however, party victories do make a difference: in the capacity of the party to "organize" the Senate and the House; in the capacity of the President to count on support on certain kinds of issues; in suggesting the general expectation of voters on the direction of public policy.

During presidential elections, the ensuing composition of the Senate and the House usually reflects in part a coattail influence; that is, the magnetic field of the Presidency attracts votes to congressional candidates running on his ticket. However, even here there are exceptions. President Eisenhower won by a smashing majority in 1956, but a Democratic majority was returned to both the Senate and the House of Representatives. In recent years, perhaps the most dramatic example of coattailing was in the election of 1964. Barry Goldwater not only lost by the largest majority in American history; he dragged down with him a sufficient number of Republican senators and congressmen to give President Johnson a Democratic majority of more than two-thirds in both Houses. Positively, many Democratic candidates were returned or elected because of the vote-getting abilities of Lyndon Johnson.

In off-year (nonpresidential) elections, the President's party has consistently lost seats in Congress. This has been true in every off-year election since the Civil War except 1934. It has been explained in part as the result of the composition of the off-year electorate: between one-fifth and one-quarter of those who vote for Presidents fail to vote in off-year congressional elections. The absence of presidential coattails is also a factor. Whatever the cause, it is disturbing to incumbent Presidents. For this reason, since 1954, it has been considered a normal presidential activity to campaign on behalf of the party's congressional candidates in off-year elections. The practice is still too recent to prove much. Certainly the off-year elections of 1958, 1962, and 1966 followed traditional patterns of out-party gains; but who is to say that the results would not have been worse without presidential participation?

Party and Personal Determinants

Political science has made great strides in the past two decades in illuminating, with the help of quantitative analysis, the voting behavior of the electorate and the peculiar asymmetries that exist between congressional behavior and constituent attitudes and interests. One of the most comprehensive studies, *Representation in Congress* by Warren Miller and Donald Stokes,[8] indicates that the overwhelming factor in voting for candidates for Congress is party identification. This does not necessarily imply that a congressman's own voting record is unimportant; but it does emphasize the fact that, in spite of splinter groups in both parties in both houses, there is a strong party cohesion on most important issues which come before the Congress. This the electorate senses vaguely at best,[9] so the explanation for what party cohesion exists must be found less in public expectation than in presidential and party leadership within the legislative system.

Miller and Stokes shed particular light on the degree to which elections "instruct" congressmen on particular issues. Except in the case of the civil rights issues in southern states and districts, most congressmen are given substantial discretion on how they vote. There seems, however, to be an expectation that on domestic issues they will conform roughly to the traditional programs, policies, and viewpoints of their national party (e.g., Democrats are generally expected to vote for extensions of public services by the federal government; Republicans, against such extensions). In the field of foreign policy, congressmen are generally free from any kind of measurable constituent pressure. The nature of contemporary international relations leads most legislators in both parties to support the President on issues which he designates as critical to national security.[10]

It is therefore safe to conclude that, on the average, if a national legislator pays attention to major constituent interests and follows his party's line on major domestic issues, he will be returned to office as long as his *party* holds the loyalty of a majority of voters in his state or district.

In closely balanced two-party states or districts, the personal charisma of a candidate may be sufficient to give him bipartisan support. How else does one explain a Margaret Chase Smith (R.) and an Edmund Muskie (D.) from Maine? an Edward Brooke (R.) and an Edward Kennedy (D.) from Massachusetts? a Clifford Case (R.) and a Harrison Williams (D.) from New Jersey? It is difficult in such cases to conclude that either party affiliation or legislative voting records are totally determinative influences on the popular mind.

The Electoral Environment

What then does the whole process mean? It means that those who make our laws in the Congress achieve their legitimacy from the fact of their receiving more votes than anyone else for their particular position. It means that congressmen must justify themselves and their record by submitting their careers to the test of election.

How do congressmen then "represent" those who elect them? This is one of the trickiest and most persistent questions in all of political science. In the eighteenth century Edmund Burke contended that the duty of a representative was not to reflect the passing judgments of his constituency but to exercise his own best judgment. Representation was "virtual" rather than "direct." He was promptly defeated at the next election, but it is unclear from the historical record whether his defeat was due to his philosophy of representation or to his constituents' judgment that his "own best judgment" was not good enough. All one can say is that in modern America, the realities of elections cause legislators to pay attention to constituent interests—at least as the particular congressman defines them. But on many, if not most, issues he is given substantial latitude in constructing a policy position compounded of direct constituent pressures, presidential and party pulls and loyalties, his own reflective judgment on the meaning of the public weal, and the anticipated consequences of his action for his advancement in the power structure of the legislative body.

What has happened in this past decade is an increasing confluence, or at least overlapping, of these several considerations. As this confluence develops, the nature of the congressional system changes from one that accommodates the gaps between parochial and national interests to one that emphasizes their commonalities.

Congressional Constituencies in Transition

There are two fundamental forces at work in modifying congressional constituencies: urbanism and the American Black. Both these forces have long affected the presidential constituency, for they are key elements in the fashioning of electoral college victories. But only recently have these forces affected a majority of states and congressional districts. As the nation becomes more urban, states and congressional districts take on increasingly the complexion of microcosms of the nation as a whole. This extends to the fact that in both presidential and congressional constituencies the urban Black is becoming more numerous and more critically important in determining the outcome of elections. Census data from 1950 to 1960 document these important generalizations. Projections of the 1970 census give further support.

Between 1950 and 1960 the number of American citizens living in urban areas rose from 96 to 125 million. Seventy percent of all Americans now live in urban places. Regionally, the urban drift is dramatic. Whereas in the Northeast (New England, Middle Atlantic, and East North Central States) urbanization increased by only 1.4 percent, the figure for the Pacific Coast and the West North Central States was almost 7 percent; for the South Atlantic States more than 8 percent; for the East South Central States more than 9 percent; and for the West South Central and the Rocky Mountain States more than 12 percent.

The simple lesson of these trends is that the areas of the United States most traditionally rural have within a decade manifested a massive shift of population into cities—especially medium-sized cities and suburbs. If the new Congress is more sympathetic to the needs of people struggling with the interdependencies of urban life than it was a short time ago, this is because an increasing number of congressional districts contain substantial urban populations.

Furthermore, in the decade from 1950 to 1960 the number of Blacks living in urban places jumped from just over 9 million to almost 14 million. This was a product both of net in-migration and of new births. The effect has been to increase both the political awareness and the political power of Blacks in virtually every state and in scores of additional congressional districts across the nation. The shift in congressional behavior on civil rights legislation, which we shall review in Chapter VI, cannot be understood apart from this development. Even with the relative easing off of dramatic civil rights legislation in the Congress since the passage of the Voting Rights Act of 1965, and in spite of the national impact of the George Wallace movement, the political gains of the American Blacks have continued to manifest themselves—especially in state and local elections, and in both the North and the South. These state and local victories are not lost upon congressmen who increasingly are forced to discover accommodations between white and Black demands and pressures. Actually, in many parts of the nation in the decade of the '70's, this is the name of the game of American politics.

Chapter II

THE ENVELOPING INTERESTS

When a national legislator thinks about the constituency that elected him, he rarely if ever sees in his mind's eye an undifferentiated mass of individual voters. He sees categories of interests. In some cases he sees only a few dominant interests. His state or district may, for example, be overwhelmingly agricultural (grazing in Wyoming; wheat in the Dakotas; cotton in Mississippi; dairying in Vermont; citrus fruits in Florida); it may have sizable populations in manufacturing (autos in Michigan; steel in Pennsylvania; electronics in Massachusetts; aircraft in Washington); it may be heavily extractive (coal in West Virginia; iron in Minnesota; silver in Colorado; oil in Texas). The total economic life of his state or district may be so dependent upon the fate of one or two categories of interests that the legislator feels obliged to throw his major energies into protecting and improving the economic viability of these crucial constituent concerns. Furthermore, his natural inclinations and instincts for political survival and service may be reinforced by campaign contributions from these same dominant interests.

But increasingly in the latter part of the twentieth century, with the metropolitanization of American life and the dramatic growth in population, states and congressional districts are becoming kaleidoscopes of variegated, overlapping, cooperating, and competing interests—economic, social, and political. As the contradictory signals from home proliferate, and constituent cues on policy collide, legislators look increasingly to the President and to the party leadership in the Congress for guidance on how to vote. On any particular issue, of course, the pressures from home may be quite clear and unambiguous. In districts, for example, in which organized labor is strong and financially active in campaigns, congressmen may be sensitive to pressure on issues in which labor has a special stake. Earl Latham reports that in 1959:

> The unions opposed the enactment of the Labor-Management Reporting and Disclosure Bill which laid certain regulations on labor unions. The bill passed, but of the 126 members of the House of Representatives who had received financial aid from unions in the campaign of 1958, 116 opposed the bill, and only 8 supported it.[1]

But on a vast number of legislative issues, labor takes no strong stand, is itself divided, or is checked in its political influence by countervailing constituent pressures. The same is true of business interests, professional interests, agricultural interests, veterans' interests, race interests, nationality interests, class interests, and so on. As each state and congressional district becomes more complex in its interest-group structure, it becomes more and more a microcosm of the entire nation. Presidential, senatorial, and congressional views of their respective constituencies become, in consequence, increasingly similar. This similarity in perception gives increased life and meaning to the President and to the national party as homogenizers and moralizers of group interests.

And transcending the competition of group interests are popular attitudes that seem to well up from ineffable sources; that become national causes in spite of the absence (or presence) of obvious lobbies; that emerge from events and, fortuitously, from the outrageous impertinence of reformers and reporters. America's reversal of policy in Vietnam, Ralph Nader's crusades on behalf of the American consumer, blue- and white-collar clamorings for tax reduction and reform, are all recent manifestations of this phenomenon. Sometimes, of course, special interests find it both possible and useful to identify with these less structured developments. If, in these circumstances, the President gives tactical leadership to congressional troops, the new cause is unbeatable.

All of this needs saying in order to place the enveloping interests in our society in their proper and contemporary perspective. The New Congress in the 1970's is inexplicable apart from these general developments in interest-group diffusion and in opinion trends that have marked the past several years.

The Positive Contributions of Interest Groups

In one of the most perceptive and eloquent passages of the Federalist Papers, James Madison wrote:

> A landed interest, a manufacturing interest, a mercantile interest, a moneyed interest, and many lesser interests, grow up of necessity in civilized nations, and divide them into different classes actuated by different sentiments and views. The regulation of these various and interfering interests forms the principal task of modern legislation and involves the spirit of party and faction in the necessary operations of government.[2]

The most impressive aspect of this statement is Madison's use of the words "necessity" and "necessary." Interest groups, he contends, "grow up of *necessity* in *civilized* nations." The regulation of these competing interests by legislatures involves the spirit of party in the "*necessary*" operations of government. To Madison interest groups were necessary to civilization, and governments were necessary to regulate them. In both a more ancient and a more modern idiom, Madison would have contended that instead of being parasites on the body politic, interest groups are the benign viruses of vaccination. They itch a bit, but they preclude smallpox.

Before proceeding to a summary description of the behavior of interest groups as part of the environment of congressional behavior, it may be well to list the positive services which interest groups perform for our society. In an article for the *Encyclopaedia Britannica* on the subject a few years ago, this author stressed the following:[3]

First, interest groups make articulate the demands, grievances, and creative ideas of the many publics which comprise a democratic order and thereby often preclude festering pockets of social unrest and group frustration.

Second, they frequently provide busy legislators with expert opinions on highly complex matters.

Third, they are mutually suspicious watch dogs who sniff out each other's subtle importunities and make these visible to preoccupied congressmen, executive officials, and the public at large.

Fourth, they serve as media for disseminating information about public issues to important segments of the community.

And fifth, they act as mediating devices within their own often variegated membership, and help thereby to lower the temperature of social conflict.

These are signal services to a free society, As we proceed in our analysis of interest groups and Congress, it may be well to keep in mind that interest groups are both causes and effects of the freedom we enjoy.

Interest Groups, Pressure Groups, and Lobbies

At the outset, it is important to clear up one possible ambiguity in the use of terms. Throughout, the term "interest group" is used interchangeably with the terms "pressure group" and "lobby." Some political scientists discriminate among the three terms on the grounds that a ladies' sewing circle is an interest group, but almost never a pressure group; and that a pressure group may be ad hoc, while a lobby is institutionalized and relatively permanent. Here, however, we shall use the terms interchangeably to refer to groups that want something from the government—positively or negatively—but do not want to be held politically responsible in the sense of direct electoral accountability. Interest groups prefer to importune those who are in office, or may be in office.

What do we know about interest groups and Congress? The answer is that we know a good deal. But we have not known what we know for very long. Presaged by a prophetic treatise by Arthur Bentley at the turn of the century, the first systematic work on the subject was written only a generation ago. In the year 1929, a young political scientist named Pendleton Herring wrote a book called *Group Representation Before Congress.* Much of what Herring wrote in 1929 is still relevant. He refers at length, for example, to the "big three" of industry, labor, and agriculture. They are still the big three, although their roles and interrelationships have been substantially modified over the years. He goes on to discuss a wide variety of professional groups, women's organizations, veterans' lobbies, and what he calls "forces of organized reform." They, or their counterparts, are still around. It is true, of course, that a few interests such as the temperance lobby are no longer influential, but almost every other category of pressure group listed by Herring is still with us. In spite of vast changes in the scope, complexity, and institutionalization of lobbying, the remarkable thing is the stability of at least the superficial pattern of pressure politics over the thirty-five years since Herring's book first appeared. Even in the military hardware field, which presently looms so large in pressure politics, Herring was constrained to write in 1929, "The aircraft industry, being dependent in large measure upon the army and navy as a market for its product of course takes an interest in national defense."[4]

About the only pressure groups visible today that were not visible to Herring in 1929 are the foreign lobbies and the state and local government lobbies. Herring could not have foreseen that, in the years since the passage of the Foreign Agents Registration Act in 1942, more than fifteen hundred agents would register as having foreign principals. Japan, alone, has had as many as thirty-two lobbyists at a time working in the United States. Contemporary Americans, who are inured to the infusive diplomacy of the modern age, take this in stride. In a world of trade, aid, and mutual defense alliances, it would be strange indeed if other nations did not attempt to influence the legislative and executive policies of the most powerful nation on earth. We indulge in a little infusion of our own in other parts of the world. But there is no reason why Herring should have indulged in social prophecy—especially in the isolationist contentment of the late 1920's.

On the domestic front, as state and local governments have become increasingly affected by grants-in-aid and other federal activities, they have predictably responded with a proliferation of part- or full-time lobbyists in Washington.[5]

And, of course, the total volume of all pressure-group activity has increased since 1929 in proportion to the increase in the number of federal policies affecting the citizenry at large.

The Major Spenders

According to the *Congressional Quarterly,* the top twenty spenders, of the slightly fewer than three hundred organizations filing lobby spending reports in the late 1960's, included: United Federation of Postal Clerks (AFL-CIO); AFL-CIO (headquarters); Council for a Liveable World; American Farm Bureau Federation; American Legion; American Trucking Assns., Inc.; United States Savings and Loan League; Record Industry Association of America, Inc.; National Federation of Independent Business, Inc.; National Housing Conference, Inc.; National Farmers Union; Brotherhood of Railway, Airline & Steamship Clerks, Freight Handlers, Express and Station Employees (AFL-CIO); National Education Association Division of State and Federal Relations; Association of Mutual Fund Plan Sponsors, Inc.; Liberty Lobby, Inc.; National Association of Home Builders of the United States; Central Arizona Project Association; National Association of Letter Carriers (AFL-CIO); American Textile Manufacturers Institute, Inc.; and National Council of Farmer Cooperatives.[6]

For some purposes this is a useful list. It suggests continuing and emerging categories of pressure politics. It suggests countervailing lobbies within single categories of group interest. Agriculture, for example, is deeply split between the conservative, free-market interests of the American Farm Bureau Federation on the one hand; and the pro-welfare-state, federal-subsidy interests of the National Farmers Union. But the list is also woefully incomplete. The lobby registration section of the Legislative Reorganization Act of 1946, as amended, and as interpreted by the United States Supreme Court, requires organizations to register as lobbies only if lobbying is their *major* function and involves "direct communication with Members of Congress." Where in the list is the National Association of Manufacturers or the U. S. Chamber of Commerce? These powerful interest groups have contended successfully that lobbying is not their major function. Hence they do not register. Catholic-dominated associations, like Citizens for Educational Freedom, have been powerful influences on federal aid-to-education bills, but there is no public record of their lobbying expenditures.

Nor are powerful lobbies always the affluent ones. Certain civil rights groups exercise extraordinary influence, not because they are well financed, but because they represent a powerful electoral and moral force in key segments of the voting public. As we have noted, scores of states, counties, and municipalities have full-time lobbyists in Washington to keep track of the welfare, health, education, highway, urban renewal, and other federal programs which mightily affect local budgets and local policies. These lobbyists seldom register.

Whether registered or not, however, lobbies are ubiquitous on the Washington landscape, and many of them are unquestionably very well financed.

The Nature of Influence

It is both easy and inaccurate to establish a simple, stimulus-response behavioral model of influence: lobbies exert pressure, congressmen knuckle under. The fact is that pressure politics in the American Congress is multi-instrumental, multi-dimensional, and multi-directional. Legislators are not neuters waiting to be played upon by any passing force. Pressure groups, like seed corn, cannot produce harvests except in fertile soil. Many years ago, referring to a conservative senator from the state of Delaware, I made the comment that it was less the pressure of the du Pont Company *upon* C. Douglas Buck than the pressure of du Pont *in* C. Douglas Buck that affected his legislative behavior. Buck was a du Pont in-law, and had grown up within the climate of opinion established by that remarkable house of industry. Senators and congressmen bring with them to Capitol Hill a whole series of predilections about social and economic issues. These philosophical attitudes stem from family, past professional associations, deferential patterns within their home constituencies, and the general ethos of the idealogical leadership which they have come over the years to respect. Washington politics is a search for friends. Initiative on behalf of a particular cause may come from inside the halls of Congress as well as from outside. Furthermore, more legislators respond favorably to group interests because they find themselves "simpatico" with them than ever respond because of threats of reprisal. Even where constituency pressures and possible political reprisals are clear, how does one sort out the motives of an individual legislator? When Senator Henry Jackson takes up cudgels on behalf of Boeing aircraft in bids for defense contracts, is it simply because if he does not do so he might be thrown out of office at the next election? Surely this explanation is more cynical than the life of politics really is. The loss of a large defense contract to Boeing may be a multi-billion dollar nightmare. It may mean thousands of unemployed, and a general dip in the economy of the entire state of Washington, to say nothing of the nationwide ripple effect upon particular subcontractors. Surely compassion and representational concern are genuine motivating forces in legislative behavior.

Obviously when this compassionate or representational interest is evident, a lobby need not stoop to tricks to gain the legislator's support. Similarly, those private interests which come closest to the national-constituency interests of the nationally representative President have a signal advantage. It is here that the electoral behavior of the public at large comes closest to true influence upon congressional behavior. Most of the great legislative decisions of the past quarter of a century in both the international and domestic welfare fields have come about because of the coincidence of presidential views of the nation's needs with fortuitous coalitions of interest group aspirations in the private sector. Neither alone would have sufficed. Together, the combination is unbeatable.

Take a recent example, beautifully documented in part by Bauer, Pool, and Dexter.[7] For a quarter of a century, American Presidents have taken the view that a liberal, low-tariff international trade policy was in the best interest of this nation's national security. This world view runs counter to the historic American concern with protectionism, and most certainly runs counter to the contemporary interests of scores of powerful private interests in the American economy. And yet, on the whole, liberal trade agreement acts are renewed whenever they come close to expiration. Presidential success in this continuing conflict is owed largely to a most elaborate symbiosis between executive interests and selected private interests. Shortly after World War II, for example, domestic watch manufacturers in the United States put on a campaign to increase tariffs on Swiss watches and parts. The lobby was well financed and astutely led. But some bright official in the Department of State hit on the notion that the prosperity of thousands of jewelry shops all over the United States might be adversely affected by higher tariffs on Swiss watches and parts. Millions of GI's had bought Swiss watches in PX's all over the globe during the War. Now back home, would the GI's and the jewelers be happy at a sudden jump in the cost of watch repair? A counterlobby was hastily organized, letters and telegrams flooded Congress from every nook and cranny of the nation, and the domestic watch companies were successfully contained. The principle of countervailing pressures in the tariff field has now reached such a fine art that even traditionally protectionist organizations like the National Association of Manufacturers find themselves so torn internally on the tariff issue that they have become effectively immobilized as a pressure group in international trade policy.

Since 1953 the most powerful force on the presidential side of tariff legislation has been the Committee for a National Trade Policy whose sole purpose it is to promote liberal trade legislation. Made up largely of American export interests which stand to lose when other nations cannot sell vigorously in the American market, CNTP works in close conjunction with the White House and with the Department of State on legislative strategy—sometimes, incidentally, at cross purposes with powerful forces in the Departments of Commerce and Agriculture, which occasionally side with selected protectionist interests in the private sector. In the 1962 trade struggle, CNTP had eight full-time staff in its Washington office in addition to a number of clerical workers. The job of CNTP is to harness the political influence of every economic group in the nation that has a direct or indirect interest in lower rather than higher tariffs. Labor, agriculture, and business find themselves split horizontally rather than vertically. Perhaps of all legislation, trade bills foster unnatural coalitions of temporary influence. Men who yell at each other across collective bargaining tables find themselves in joyous partnership on tariff questions—as they do on defense contracts.

In recent years, an interesting alignment of interest groups has taken place vis-à-vis federal fiscal policy. Business interests have become notably relaxed about federal tax reductions and budget deficits during periods of economic decline and substantial unemployment. This marks a major shift in business attitudes from those obtaining in the 1940's and 1950's. In fact, by the end of the Kennedy administration, virtually every major constellation of group interests in the nation had accepted the essentially Keynesian notion that federal deficit financing was an appropriate means of stimulating the national economy.

But no such agreement exists when the economic issue is inflation rather than slump. On the subject of how best to cool an overheated economy even economists are split—although a majority would agree that some combination of high interest rates, high taxes, lower government spending, and national-debt reduction is the necessary road away from spiraling prices. Bankers and businessmen tend to agree, though the latter will struggle to insure that reductions in federal spending do not adversely affect particular commercial or industrial contracts.

But organized labor disagrees—correctly relating government-induced deflation to the prospect of mounting unemployment, and sharing with the nation's non-union middle class a growing dismay at high taxes that (through exemptions) favor the rich, on the one hand, and (through welfare payments) support indigent poor, on the other.

And religious and reform groups disagree—believing that increased federal spending for the sick, the poor, and the ignorant is a matter of top priority if the major pathologies and injustices in our society are ever to be overcome.

And state and local governments disagree—as they look to the federal government for additional spending in order to create (by substitution) some measure of tax relief for state and local taxpayers.

These three major categories of "disagreers" either reject certain ingredients in the anti-inflation medicine, or they make strident demands upon the federal government to cut spending in what they regard as "non-people" or "anti-people" programs (e.g. space, defense). They also press for anti-inflation policies that do not create a massive inequality in the degree of sacrifice from various groups (e.g. bankers getting rich while those on welfare are hurt and unemployment increases).

The politics of inflation is intriguing and complicated, and is little understood. In group-interest terms, it is far more difficult to analyze and to predict than the politics of depression where virtual unanimity about policy presently obtains. The politics of the 1970's will see both inflationary and deflationary movements in the economy, but most forecasters predict more of the former than of the latter.

The Techniques of Lobbying

How do pressure groups actually ply their trade? What does lobbying the Congress actually involve in this day and age?

Again there is no simple answer. Straight bribery and personal payoffs are not, alas, unknown, but they are rarer than occasional scandals make them appear. Most lobbyists work a legitimate game, even if the game at times involves artful indirection. Certainly the most obvious and innocent lobbying activity is presenting oral or written statements to congressional committees or to individual members of Congress. The good lobbyist never intentionally distorts. He simply puts facts in a friendly light. As Douglass Cater has quoted in his analysis of *Power in Washington,* "the cardinal sin is to supply faulty information which puts a trusting policy-maker in an exposed position."[8]

But lobbyists obviously do not stop with direct lobbying. They buttress their Washington activities with all kinds of grass roots activities and with lateral negotiations with other lobbies in Washington and in the field. Some of them publish and circularize the voting records of legislators to constituents back home, usually evaluating the voting records in terms of "right" votes and "wrong" votes, in the hopes of arousing the support or wrath of powerful segments of the voting population. Some pressure groups maintain an elaborate list of hometown bigwigs who are personally friendly to, or at least influential with, important congressmen and senators. Through a series of fences, these key members of local power elites are approached to put personal pressure upon the legislator. It is not hard for a congressman to discount impersonal mass mailings obviously inspired by an enterprising lobbyist. It is quite another thing to discount a personal phone call or visitation from the president of the local bank, or an old friend who also happens to be the vice chairman of the local cooperative committee.

Lobbyists also work on and through the bureaucracy. With the increase in importance of the executive branch in legislative initiative, the cultivation of the minds of key policy-makers in the various federal departments and agencies is often the precondition of pressure group success in the Congress. It is also the key to influencing the decisions of executive branch personnel in implementing laws once enacted.

Finally, big lobbying today gets into the heart of the partisan political process. It does so through elaborate public relations techniques and through providing money and services for the political campaigns of friendly legislators. Much of this is aboveboard, but some of it lacks public visibility and suffers the moral ambiguity of all devious activity. For instance, anyone who has studied carefully the public relations techniques of the American Medical Association in its bitter struggle against National Health Insurance in the late 1940's and early 1950's can only be fascinated by and appalled at the moral sleaziness of a usually noble profession.[9] Where facts were not on their side, innuendoes sufficed. Articles were ghosted, planted, and reprinted so that the reader had no notion that it was the A.M.A. public relations staff at work. Anyone who supported that triumph of Madison Avenue invective, "socialized medicine," was subjected to sustained political denigration by the American Medical Political Action Committee—the political arm of the Association. Candidates friendly to the A.M.A. position received both money and public relations services during their campaigns.

A.M.A. has not been alone in these kinds of activities, but its work has been dramatic and well documented. The passage of the Medicare Bill in 1965 over violent A.M.A. opposition testifies to the limits of this kind of pressure when presidential and party programs work through the new Congress. The continuing power of the A.M.A., however, was once again demonstrated in 1969 when it reputedly blocked the appointment of Dr. John H. Knowles as Assistant Secretary of HEW for Health and Scientific Affairs.

Labor organizations are influential both in their campaign spending and in their provision of various campaign services which are in a sense a surrogate for money. Friendly legislators are provided with campaign workers and ward canvassers. Transportation mobilized by the unions carries voters to the polls on election days. Union journals publicize the activities and statements of legislative friends. Union members sign letters-to-the-editor written by union headquarters. And, of course, union-sponsored "voluntary" campaign funds are frequently provided to sympathetic candidates.

Business-oriented interests have been slow to react to labor's political activities, but in 1963 an organization was formed called BIPAC—Business-Industry Political Action Committee. According to Charles

Clapp, "BIPAC . . . is bipartisan in nature, intends to restrict its efforts to congressional races, and will provide financial aid for candidates who will support 'sound fiscal policies and who uphold the free, private, and competitive system.' "[10] Various conservative groups have, of course, carried on similar but disjointed activities of this kind in the past. BIPAC has turned out to be a far more unified and sustained instrument of pressure politics than any of its predecessors. In recent years, BIPAC has, according to its own official reports, collected and spent in the neighborhood of $300,000 per election year to support congressional candidates who agree with its philosophy.

Assessment

These competing attempts to capture the mind of the public, the support of the bureaucracy, and the vote of the legislator, are important manifestations of the never-ending conflicts which democracy must resolve peacefully. No one group interest can dominate the entire legislative field, although certain group interests in certain specialized areas are sufficiently powerful to warrant Douglass Cater's label of "sub-governments."[11] To be a true "sub-government," a pressure group must be sufficiently rich, sufficiently specialized, and sufficiently well connected to sources of abiding power in the structure of Congress and the structure of executive bureaus to withstand countervailing pressures of containment by the general forces of President and party. Such sub-governments do exist: sugar, oil, and certain defense manufactures come to mind. So do the private interests that influence tax legislation generally.[12] But "sub-governments" are the exception rather than the rule in the United States, and even some of the most entrenched bastions of privilege are finding their traditional positions threatened. An aroused nation, for example, has finally induced Congress to begin the process of chipping away at the tax exemptions of, and the tax benefits to, traditionally favored industries and individuals.

The rule, actually, is increasingly a hopeful one—friendly to the evolving institutions of a complex democracy. For the story of pressure groups and Congress is more than a tale of blind armies clashing by night. It is far more than the sleazy story of influence-peddling which we will explore in Chapter VIII. Instead, it is generally the story of the moralizing and the homogenizing of group interests through a system of political accountability. The system is complex and imperfect, but its total effect is to produce public policies which on the whole are beneficial to the welfare of the majority of citizens. Not the least reason for this is that most important legislative proposals today come not from group interests, but from the President of the United States.

Chapter III

THE PERVASIVE EXECUTIVE

If congressmen are influenced in their behavior by elections and by group interests, they are also influenced mightily by the activities and programs of the President and the executive departments and agencies. There are reasons for not saying "the President and *his* executive departments and agencies." The executive branch is not a neat pyramid of organization with the President at the top. It is a highly decentralized operation with a number of semiautonomous parts, and with most of its decisions ambiguously accountable both to the President and to parts of the Congress.

But taken together, the President and the executive departments and agencies are a major force in congressional life. The executive branch impinges on almost everything Congress does. Basically, it sets the legislative agenda in most fields; it rides herd on bills designated as important by the President who also possesses the whip of a possible veto; it largely dominates national security policy; its day-to-day decisions affect the economy and the personal lives of citizens in every congressional district in the United States. So substantial in fact have become its powers and activities that some students of public affairs have become frightened. Their fear is that a continuing accretion of presidential and executive branch power will make Congress into a rubber stamp, and that the United States will end up with a Caesarian-technocratic government unfriendly to freedom.

This seems an exaggerated fear. In the image of wrestling, if the executive branch has some holds on the Congress, the Congress has some "half-Nelsons," "scissors," and "toe-holds" of its own. It may be reassuring to note that in American history, it has been rare for one branch to pin the other branch to the mat. In actual fact, the metaphor is misleading. For the only appropriate image is not two-way wrestling, but "gang" wrestling: three-way, four-way, six-way. To pretend that the major conflicts in the federal government are those between the President and the Congress is to simplify reality to the point of distortion. Portions of interlocking power exist in many corners of the government. It is not a rare phenomenon to have one team of "wrestlers" made up of a congressman, a well-placed bureau chief, and a powerful outside interest group. These may be pitted in the ring against another team made up of the President, his budget director, and an opposing interest group; or a senator, another bureau chief, and a league of municipalities. If on a lonely Saturday morning a congressman feels overwhelmed by the power of the President and the federal bureaucracy, there are a score of executive branch officials who at that very moment are pondering the power of Congress or some key section thereof. Presidents may set budgets, but how many parts of those budgets have been prepared at the agency level with someone's eye on past or possible future congressional reactions?

Whatever else can be said about the Washington scene, it is not neat. The centers of power are many; the patterns of cooperation and conflict are loose and ill-defined. They are also tentative. The first session of the 89th Congress was so friendly to President Johnson's legislative agenda as to create concern that Congress had become too permissive, too deferential. By the end of the Johnson administration, Congress was in an ugly mood toward the President. And President Nixon's relations with the 91st Congress involved such a series of legislative cliff-hangers, compromises, and rejections as to raise once again in the minds of many thoughtful people the question of whether our complex constitutional system is consonant with the demands of the latter third of the twentieth century. For reasons close to the theme of this book, the secular trend is toward a closer coincidence of presidential and congressional views on important public policies. But the unities will emerge from a vast and continuing pluralism which has always marked our national political and governmental life.

The central point is that this kaleidoscope of power must increasingly be placed in the context of presidential influence. What he proposes to Congress, and his success in harnessing the strengths of the disparate units theoretically under him in the executive branch, have unquestionably a major effect upon congressional behavior.

The Presidential Initiative

Richard Neustadt has referred in his writings to "the very senior chairman of a major House committee [who] reportedly admonished an administration witness, 'Don't expect us to start from scratch on what you people want. That's not the way we do things here—*you* draft the bills and *we* work them over.' "[1]

There is, of course, no constitutional mandate that bills must be drafted by the executive branch. All the Constitution says on this subject is that the President "shall from time to time give to the Congress information of the state of the Union, and recommend to their consideration such measures as he shall judge necessary and expedient. . . . " If the executive branch now exercises a virtual monopoly on the drafting of major bills, it is because the complex agenda of modern public policy necessitates an expertise and a coordination which only the executive branch can provide.

Actually what is really new is not that executive departments and agencies work with congressmen (and pressure groups) in developing and refining legislative proposals. This has always been true to some extent. What is new is the *degree* of reliance on presidential initiative and the role of the President's office in imposing a measure of order and coordination on the process of legislative initiative and follow-through. No better illustration exists of the dependence of Congress upon Presidential initiative than the behavior of the 91st Congress during the first few months of the Nixon administration. By previous standards, Nixon was slow in developing a legislative program. The 91st Congress under opposition-party leadership, instead of striking out on its own, fidgeted and did almost nothing for six months.

This situation is, of course, unusual, and occurs only when a new President takes over. Normally the legislative program of the President—at least in dramatic outline—appears in three formal messages submitted to the Congress each January: the State of the Union message, the budget message, and the economic report. The first of these is the most inclusive and, politically, the most important. The President delivers it in person to the two Houses seated together. If a bomb were to fall on the House chamber at the instant of the President's State of the Union message, all of the top personnel in the United States government would be wiped out—President, Vice President, cabinet members, senators, congressmen, Supreme Court justices, and top military brass, to say nothing of scores of ambassadors and other dignitaries in the gallery. For they are all present, so important is the State of the Union message considered to be. Along with the President's Inaugural address, the State of the Union message is considered the Chief Executive's major instrument for articulating the general goals of his administration.

The budget message, of course, presents the dollars and cents of the recommended program. The economic report, mandated by the Employment Act of 1946, summarizes general economic conditions and recommends measures aimed at maintaining "maximum employment, production, and purchasing power."

These three messages, all coming to Congress in January of each year, begin the process of narrowing the legislative agenda and of establishing legislative priorities. But increasingly the three messages are followed by a series of special messages in particular areas of public policy, usually accompanied by bill drafts. Even though President Nixon did not present a comprehensive State of the Union message to Congress in the early months of his incumbency, he did submit a series of special legislative messages on subjects as diverse as government reorganization, tax reform, organized crime, consolidation of grants-in-aid, District of Columbia reorganization, food for the poor, foreign aid, ABM, postal reform, airport development, broadened unemployment insurance, the draft, drug abuse, population control, and welfare reform. Such messages are usually accompanied (or followed) by drafts of specific bills, and are sometimes reinforced with letters submitted to legislative leaders urging action on a series of specific items.

The issuance of a presidential message or letter or bill draft is, of course, only that part of the legislative initiative which is visible. Prior to, and subsequent to, the submission of such messages and documents, the presidential entourage is busily engaged in their preparation or implementation. On the preparatory side, the lion's share of the work is carried by individual departments and agencies—aided, abetted, guided, and sometimes thwarted by the Office of Legislative Reference in the United States Bureau of the Budget, and by key presidential aides in the White House. The Office of Legislative Reference assumes the major responsibility for insuring that legislative proposals emanating from the several departments and agencies of the federal government are, in fact, in "accord with the program of the President." The White House aides restyle and redraft messages and bills in line with presidential suggestions. In some cases, a Cabinet-White House team is the effective agent of legislative innovation. For example, the Moynihan-Finch team was credited with the historic welfare-reform package submitted to Congress by President Nixon in August 1969.

Since virtually every piece of legislation has a price tag, the development of legislative proposals must be dovetailed intimately and inextricably with the preparation of the President's budget message to Congress. Ever since 1921, the President has had prepared annually a consolidated executive branch budget for submission to the Congress. Ever since the Truman administration, the preparation of the annual budget and the development of the President's legislative agenda have been part of a single process of program planning. Twelve to eighteen months prior to any particular fiscal year (July 1-June 30), a call goes out from the Bureau of the Budget to each federal department and agency. The call is for estimates of expenditures for the fiscal year in question, and for any legislation which the department or agency wishes to propose. An elaborate process of intra- and inter-agency bargaining and clearance ensues. Clearance with key congressmen may also be involved. The net result is that the three major presidential messages delivered in January, plus special presidential messages, plus specific bill drafts submitted from time to time, constitute an elaborate procedure for coordination and priority-setting by the executive office of the President. When an occasional bill is drafted in the Congress, outside of this context, it can risk the danger of presidential veto (or inattention) if it has not at an early stage cleared the Bureau of the Budget.

Congressmen are constantly aware of the legislative powers of the President. However much attention a congressman may give to constituent errands, he knows that his *legislative* performance will be judged by what he does with the bill drafts submitted by the President of the United States. The scorekeepers of legislative performance (the press, the *Congressional Quarterly News Service,* lobbies, etc.) use the President's legislative agenda as the basis of their evaluations and tallies. Such evaluations can and do find their way into constituents' hands.

The President, then, is an omnipresent force in congressional life. In legislative terms, it is *his* view of national necessity which is overriding in setting the congressional agenda. It is his power of veto which threatens the passage of legislation he himself has not sponsored or endorsed. In many areas of foreign affairs and national security policy, his prerogatives and constitutional authorities have at times been so substantial as to make Congress little more than a shadow or an echo. This last deserves elaboration.

The President and Foreign Affairs

Theoretically, Congress has an arsenal of constitutional weapons in the field of foreign affairs and national security. It has the authority to "regulate the value . . . of foreign coins," "define . . . offences against the Law of Nations," "declare war," "raise and support armies," "provide and maintain a Navy," "make rules for the government and regulation of the land and naval forces," "provide for calling forth the militia to . . . repel invasions." In addition, the Senate has power of confirmation of appointments of cabinet members, ambassadors, and military officers. It also has the power, by a two-thirds vote, to share in the treaty-making power of the President. Finally, Congress appropriates all monies to be spent on foreign as well as on domestic affairs.

But in virtually all these matters, Congress until recently has deferred in large measure to presidential judgment. The justification was persuasive. Only the President, it was reasoned, had the sources of intelligence, the unity of command, and the ability to act with the necessary dispatch in the day-to-day conduct of national security policy. Furthermore, the President could mobilize public opinion swiftly, and usually sympathetically, behind his foreign policy stands and actions. Television, radio, and press were at his beck and call. The advent of nuclear weapons and missile technology, it was held, simply speeded up a process which had been developing for more than half a century—of placing major responsibility for foreign and military affairs in the hands of the President and his major executive subordinates.

In some areas, like foreign aid, agricultural surplus disposal, tariffs, import quotas, the disposal of domestic military bases, and immigration policy, ten major committees of Congress, fifteen minor committees, and scores of subcommittees (and their respective staffs and chairmen) have had substantial influence over policy decisions for some time. But on the large issues of troop commitments, overall military budgets, choice of investments in expensive military hardware, appropriate responses to international threats, the size and location of overseas bases, and the fine print in international executive agreements and defense pacts, these same committees and subcommittees, until recently, have been largely passive and supportive of presidential policies.

As a result of Vietnam, the pendulum has begun to shift. In the 91st Congress, President Nixon's Anti-Ballistic Missile (ABM) program passed the Senate with the margin of a single vote—the closest vote on a matter of importance to national security in more than a quarter of a century.

The weakening of the President's role in national security affairs must not, however, be overstated. His power and authority in matters of foreign policy and national defense policy are still enormous and are especially evident in his marshalling of arguments, evidence, and opinion behind specific legislative proposals in these crucial areas of national concern.

Once again the point to be made is the pre-eminent role of the executive branch in policy initiative. This initiative is especially marked in the field of national security affairs, but it is observable in most other areas of public policy, domestic as well as foreign. For as the agenda of government becomes increasingly complex and specialized, Congress must depend in substantial measure upon the technical advice it receives from executive branch economists, scientists, and engineers in the making of public policy.

There are respects in which Congress plays a more positive legislative role. Such questions as fiscal policy, the dollar drain, space exploration, atomic energy production, and military hardware have constituent consequences which it is the business of Congress to ferret out. And, as we shall have reason to note in Chapter V, some parts of Congress frequently go far beyond a passive role in influencing presidential and executive agency policies and decisions. It is fair to say, however, that the major legislative role of Congress is in "working over" the bills submitted by the executive branch. The initiative, and most of the technical detail of legislation, must come from the President.

The President and the Legislative Schedule

The same is true of legislative priorities and of the struggle to get bills passed. The real test of presidential leadership is not how many measures he submits to the Congress, but how many bills which he has identified as top priority actually come back to his desk, in some recognizable form, for signature.

In building consent and support for his priority agenda, a President has a sizable tool kit of instruments. His success in using this tool kit with finesse and versatility is one of his main claims to greatness, but it also, without question, involves the most difficult of all presidential arts. All the Presidents in this century have experienced such difficulties. Woodrow Wilson met with great success in domestic legislation, but failed dismally in foreign affairs. F.D.R. was handed the reins of government for one hundred days, but following his second election, he was blocked and balked on most domestic legislation. At one point during World War II, Roosevelt got his legislative way only by threatening to act by executive fiat. Truman had a brilliant record with Congress in foreign affairs but a dismal record on domestic issues. Eisenhower found his own legislative party so divided that he had to build his legislative record with the assistance of the opposition leadership, with all of the concessions and bargains that this assistance implies. Kennedy stirred the people but never mastered the Congress. Johnson's virtuosity and strong partisan support made the 89th Congress a memorable one in the field of domestic legislation, but his magic vanished as the dreary months of the war in Vietnam rolled on. Nixon's honeymoon with Congress was short-lived. Even with secular social forces increasingly bringing presidential and congressional perspectives into focus, a President must continually build consent on "the Hill." Congress, as we shall see in the next chapter, functions by coalition, and to a certain extent, a new coalition must be found for each bill.

Success in harnessing Congress to the President's program is conditioned by many factors. One, of course, is the margin of his own victory at the polls. Unquestionably the fact that President Kennedy won by a plurality of only 112,803 votes, President Johnson by almost 16,000,000 votes, and President Nixon by a margin of only 224,197 votes, helped to determine congressional responses to the three men. Equally important is the margin of victory of the President's party in the legislative branch. The Democratic-Republican ratios in the Congresses elected in 1960, 1964, and 1968 were as follows:

	Democrats	*Republicans*	*Democratic Plurality of Congressional Seats*
1961 House	263	174	89
1961 Senate	64	36	28
1965 House	295	140	155
1965 Senate	68	32	36
1969 House	243	192	51
1969 Senate	58	42	16

The increased margin of Democratic seats in 1964 gave President Johnson a party (and an ideological) base in the Congress unavailable to his predecessor, President Kennedy. And President Nixon, of course, was faced with a Congress under the control of the opposition party.

Party loyalty is certainly not the only determinant of voting behavior in the Congress. But as Warren Miller and Donald Stokes have concluded in their elaborate and sophisticated study of "Constituency Influence in Congress,"[2] party identification is the overwhelming factor in electing congressmen to office, and at least on domestic issues (except civil rights), party regularity is high in both houses of Congress.

The power of individual committee and subcommittee chairmen can be a thorn in the President's side, even when his party commands a substantial majority in both houses. When powerfully placed congressmen or senators stand in the President's way, he has three alternatives: (1) to threaten them; (2) to educate and cajole them; (3) to let them have their way. Most Presidents prefer the second choice, and settle for a compromise with the third. The first alternative is not always real. A congressman may be effectively isolated from the consequences of presidential threats. He may not need presidential patronage or spoils to secure his nomination or election. Even if he is in need of a presidential favor, the favor once granted under duress may build resistance and hostility for the future.

For these reasons, Presidents attempt to win support by a variety of educative and personal techniques. The efforts are largely directed to key party and committee members and to any dissident or wavering legislators whose votes could swing the balance. First of all, Presidents entertain socially. Entertainment is a powerful force in the building of congressional support. As early as the first Congress, President Washington found it helpful to entertain key congressmen who did not see eye-to-eye with him.* A congressman knows that a breakfast at the White House is lively copy for his news bulletin to constituents. "Last Wednesday morning, when I was breakfasting at the White House, I told the President . . . " is a powerful "image builder." From the President's point of view, a White House breakfast is an opportunity not only to build a congressman's status with his constituents, but to educate him on the merits of a particular bill or policy stand. At the White House, congressmen "listen" as well as "talk" for their breakfast. For secure congressmen, who need no general "image building" with their constituents, a surprise presidential visit by helicopter at a family wedding or a garden party can be a powerful incentive for the congressman at least to listen to the President on the next round of public policy. A personal letter, a birthday greeting, a jointly posed picture, a telephone call—all are instruments of persuasion at the disposal of the President. But they can hardly be used constantly on all 535 legislators preoccupied with scores of bills. Although a President concentrates such attention on a few key congressmen, the job is still too big for one man.

The Institutionalization of Presidential Influence

Over the past twenty years the President's role as persuader and educator of Congress has gradually become delegated, decentralized, and (if there is such a word) recentralized. As far back as the Truman administration, the President gave ad hoc responsibilities to major cabinet officers to ride herd on important bills in Congress. Actually, throughout our history Presidents have used selected agents to help them achieve their purposes in the Congress. The post-World War II period has been unique in the sense that the business of government has so expanded that executive-legislative branch relations have had to be institutionalized. Every major department and agency now has a congressional liaison office, whatever the formal title assigned to the function. The job of the liaison officer is in part to serve the interests of Congress and congressmen by facilitating communications between the Hill and a particular department or agency. Increasingly, however, the liaison officer has become a "lobbying" arm of the President. Beginning in the Eisenhower administration, congressional relations throughout the executive branch were formalized under the coordinating supervision of the White House. The basic pattern was created by Bryce Har-

*Haynes recounts the contretemps between President Washington and certain senators, including Senator Maclay, who were delaying senatorial consent to a treaty. Senator Maclay's account of the episode starts with his declaration that the President "wishes to tread on the necks of the Senate" and ends with a detailed description of a state dinner at the White House. George H. Haynes, *The Senate of the United States* (Boston: Houghton Mifflin Company, 1938), Vol. I, p. 66.

low, Special Assistant for Legislation in the Eisenhower administration. The system was elaborated by Lawrence O'Brien, under both Kennedy and Johnson, and elaborated still further by Bryce Harlow who returned under President Nixon to fill the legislative post in the White House.

The Nixon congressional liaison system works as follows. Every Friday evening, congressional liaison officers from all major departments and agencies of the government file reports with Harlow's office. These reports cover the department's activity with Congress for the previous week as well as its projections for the coming week. On Saturday mornings, the legislative specialists of the twelve cabinet departments and of key agencies meet in the Executive Office building to discuss mutual legislative problems and overall legislative strategy and tactics. A report of these Saturday morning sessions is prepared for the President prior to his Tuesday morning meetings in the White House with Republican congressional leaders. (On occasion, especially when major problems of national security and foreign affairs are involved, President Nixon invites Democratic leaders as well. But normally the President communicates with the majority leader in the Senate and the Speaker of the House through the Republican minority leadership.)

In addition to organizing and maintaining these weekly schedules, Bryce Harlow's office sends daily reports to the President on congressional relations at five o'clock each evening. It also digests the *Congressional Record* for the President's attention each morning.

The import of all this was summed up a few years ago by Lawrence O'Brien:

> By giving coherence and structure to what had once been a series of informal, haphazard arrangements . . . the White House has ensured that [executive branch] activities would be properly channeled for maximum results and we would not have cross-wires and individuals going off in separate directions and working with Congress.[3]

The President does not have to rely on executive agency liaison alone in his attempts to educate and persuade Congress. As we noted in Chapter II, much important legislation results from the coincidence of a presidential viewpoint with that of private interest groups. In such instances lobbies can perform signal liaison services for the President and the executive branch. Chapter II also noted that influential constituents could be effective persuaders of congressmen.

It would be a mistake to assume that the final result of this elaborate game of tactics is a continuous exercise of arm twisting. As mentioned earlier, educating and cajoling are the major techniques of persuasion, whether used by the President personally or by any of his liaison agents or executive personnel. It must be emphasized again that this kind of operation can and does involve discussion of the merits of a proposal and genuine attempts to persuade congressmen to the presidential point of view. These efforts are reinforced through the weekly strategy meetings between the President and his party leaders in Congress. Oftentimes it is necessary for liaison agents or party leaders to continue their persuasion right down to the line. One can observe them buttonholing key congressmen in the corridors as the final vote is being taken.

Frequently the velvet gloves of persuasion cover a mailed fist. If one adds together the number of departments and agencies which have substantial programs in each congressional district, and if one calculates the discretionary authority necessarily delegated to the President and other executive branch officials in implementing these programs, the result is a formula for inducing many congressmen and senators not to cross the President too often.

Announcements of departmental activities that will benefit a congressional district or a state are routinely made through relevant congressmen and senators of the President's party, whether or not these legislators have had anything to do with the executive decision. The hidden side of that coin is the discretion of the executive branch to withhold innovations that a congressman would be proud to announce: a new post office, a new road, a new defense contract, a new veterans' hospital, new public housing, an educational grant. The list of innovations is long and increasingly impressive in its potential for presidential power and party discipline.

The struggle is far from one-sided, however. An agency is not likely to deny a congressman a legitimate plum if the result would be a massive retribution against the agency in the next appropriations round. Furthermore, a President can twist arms once too often; and sometimes this leads congressmen to invoke "separation of powers." When congressional tempers snap they snap noisily. Backed by the largest congressional majority in the nation's history, and using the famous arm-twisting tactics of Corcoran and Cohen, President Roosevelt in 1937 was unable to press through Congress his Supreme Court packing plan. President Johnson certainly had his "comeuppances." So has President Nixon. In short, the rule of the day has been, and will continue to be, persuasion rather than coercion.

Whatever the tactics and the forces on the presidential or the congressional side, the basic fact is still that the initiative, the priority setting, and the continuing legislative leadership are now massively and preponderantly in the hands of the President. This is a fact which every congressman recognizes as a major condition of his working political environment. In the field of legislation it is the major element in the ecology of congressional behavior. It is a central fact in the operation of the new Congress in the 1970's.

Chapter IV

CENTRIPETAL FORCES: PARTY LEADERSHIP AND ORGANIZATION

The most fundamental question that can be asked about any social system is "What are its purposes?" The purposes of the United States Congress are complex and manifold. Some are clear and overt; some are obscure and hidden. But unless an attempt is made to define the goals of the congressional system, questions of organization and leadership become unmanageable. The difficulty is, of course, that congressional goals are changing, and that as these goals change, so does the structure of the system. Even so, certain continuing purposes can be identified.

At the highest level of abstraction, the purpose of the congressional system is to fulfill the duties imposed upon it by the letter and the spirit of the Constitution: to legitimate norms, to resolve conflict peacefully, to check the abuse of power, and to promote the national security and general welfare. In middle-level, instrumental terms, the purpose of the congressional system is to do these things by procedures that are orderly, deliberate, and conducive to institutional continuity. At the level of personal goals, the purpose of the congressional system is to achieve its broad societal and instrumental interests while maintaining the status and advantage of those who share in top congressional influence.

That these various purposes are not always consonant with one another should not mislead us into believing that they are fundamentally incompatible. To the contrary, unless a system satisfies both external expectations and internal desires, it cannot possibly survive over time. In the short run, external expectations and internal desires may be at odds. In the long run, they must achieve a stable coherence if the system is to endure.

As we have noted, constituent voters, group interests, and the Presidency are the major formulators of external expectations. They constitute the *exogenous* inputs into the congressional system. Congress is organized and led in part to satisfy these external interests—interests which, because they themselves are frequently at odds, Congress must help to integrate. Congress is also organized to promote the careers and to maintain the status of those who hold effective influence in its several parts. These personal designs constitute an important segment of the *functional relations* within the congressional system.

The dynamics of congressional behavior—the underlying reasons for existing patterns of congressional organization, leadership, and procedures—are to be found in the tensions among and between exogenous inputs and functional relations. That is, the system exists to achieve the multiple expectations represented by both external and internal purposes. As these purposes are redefined and modified, the system (i.e., the relationship of components) changes. So do its outputs.

Party and Coalition

To achieve its internal and external purposes, Congress for historic reasons organizes by party, but operates on matters of substance by a series of coalitions, in committee and on the floor. In normative terms, the test of responsible politics is whether coalitions are based on a majority from the party that has *organized* the Congress or one house thereof. If so, it is a benign coalition, since structural and functional power are roughly coterminous. When the party that organizes power cannot deliver it, an inverted coalition is at work. What has been wrong with the conservative coalition of the past generation is not that it was conservative, but that except for two sessions of Congress it was, in terms of political responsibility, inverted. The party that organized each house could not dominate the coalition that set its substantive record. Because of the reapportionment decisions of the Supreme Court, dramatic diminutions in the power of Southern Democrats, and other fundamental forces at work in the society, it is probable that benign coalitions will dominate the next twenty-five years of congressional life, just as inverted coalitions have dominated the past twenty-five years.

"Organizing by party and voting by coalition" explains a great deal about the nature of leadership in the Congress. Leaders must be loyal partisans with a flair for negotiating with the opposition, partisan and substantive. The effect of these twin necessities of partisan organization and substantive coalitions is to produce a spirit of compromise and accommodation in the deliberations of Congress which does much to promote civility and fundamental unity in our national life. If coalitions are benign, they do not destroy the basic notion of partisan accountability at the polls, and deviations from party policy are not harmful. Most Americans have a clear idea of the policy tendencies of Democratic and Republican majorities in the Congress; and individual constituencies understand the effective reason for any deviations from these partisan tendencies. When a Richard Russell (D., Georgia) votes with the Republican majority, or a Jacob Javits (R., New York) votes with a Democratic majority, they cancel each other's votes without disturbing the general notion of party responsibilty, if the remaining coalition is benign.

Viewed in this light, it is fair to say that regardless of who had the formal power to organize the two houses of Congress from 1938 to 1964, a conservative partnership was in substantive control of the Congress, and it achieved its purposes, by and large, through an inverted coalition. During the first term of the Johnson administration, the Democratic party was in control of Congress, achieving its substantive majority through a "benign" coalition. The election of 1966 led to a partial reversion to an inverted coalition. At this writing, it is still too early to pass judgment on the performance of the 91st Congress. But it is safe to predict that on many domestic issues liberal Democrats and moderate Republicans will coalesce to support the President. In opposition will be those Southern Democrats and conservative Republicans who, for years, made up the inverted coalition that dominated Congress.

The Need for Organization

Understanding the organization and leadership in each house is not a simple exercise. Not only do the two houses organize separately and differently; so do the two parties in each house. But in broad outline, both houses and both parties must organize to meet similar and immediate needs. These needs can be put in the form of questions:

—who is to determine who will hold formal leadership positions?
—who is to determine who will serve on the various standing committees?
—who is to control the order in which bills are considered on the floor?
—who is to control the nature and extent of floor debate?
—who is to appoint conferees to iron out the differences in bills as passed by the Senate and House?
—who is to take the responsibilty for lining up partisan or coalition majorities?

——who is to allocate partisan money for campaign contributions?

In an attempt to answer these and other questions, Congress has developed a series of partisan gatherings, committees, and offices. Caucus, conference, policy committee, rules committee, steering committee, committee on committees, campaign committee, Speaker, President pro tem, majority leader, minority leader, whip—all of these refer to instruments of organization and leadership in one or both parties of one or both houses of Congress.

Only three congressional offices are specifically provided for in the Constitution: the Speaker of the House, the Vice President (as President of the Senate), and a President pro tempore, in the absence of the Vice President. The Constitution does, however, provide for each house to "choose . . . other officers," although nothing is said about how the choice is to be made.

Of these constitutional offices of the Congress, only the choice of Vice President is made outside of the system itself. Partly because of this fact, the Vice President has traditionally had little influence in the Senate, except on the occasion of a tie which he is constrained to break.

The other two constitutional officers, the President pro tem and the Speaker of the House, along with the majority party and minority party leaders in both houses, are chosen by the basic instrument of party organization in the Congress: the caucus. The four partisan caucuses, or conferences, made up of respective party members in each house, gather at the beginning of each Congress to elect their respective officers. The caucus also endorses or modifies the recommendations of its committee on committees for the assignment of members to the various standing committees in each House.

Once leadership is identified in caucus, the stage is set for the formal ratification of party decisions by the respective chambers. By tradition, votes on organization are strictly by party lines. Also, by tradition, the President pro tem of the Senate is the man with the greatest seniority in the majority party in that chamber. Neither he nor the Vice President spends much time as presiding officer, however. This chore is reserved, by and large, for freshman senators.

The Speaker

The presiding officer of the House presents another picture altogether. The Speaker occupies the most powerful single office in the Congress. He combines majority party leadership with the traditional parliamentary responsibility of impartial umpire. Except when the House dissolves into a Committee of the Whole for purposes of reworking legislation prior to House consideration, the Speaker is expected to preside. He also—along with his staff, the majority leader, and the party whips—is expected to provide the majority party membership with a party line on important issues. In this role he becomes an important broker between the President of the United States and the majority party membership in the House of Representatives. He is never totally the President's man; he is never totally the instrument of the majority party; he is never totally the impartial umpire of the whole House. And yet to a degree he is all of these things. His success as a Speaker is related to his capacity to play these diverse and sometimes divergent roles with integrity and skill, and to negotiate honorably and flexibly with the minority party leadership on matters affecting "both sides of the aisle."

Powerful as the role of Speaker presently is, it is a pale shadow of what it once was. In the late nineteenth and twentieth centuries, under "Czars" like Reed and Cannon, the Speaker was a virtual dictator of House appointments and House business. A bipartisan revolt in 1910, led by George Norris and Robert LaFollette, reduced the Speaker's powers and left him with little more than the opportunity to compete and cooperate with other centers of authority in the House (notably the Rules Committee and the majority Committee on Committees) for the exercise of effective influence. Even so, the Speaker is not without some power in his own right, especially over procedures.

As Richard Fenno has written:

> He must recognize any member who wishes to speak on the floor; he rules on the appropriateness of parliamentary procedures; he determines the presence of a quorum; he selects the Chairman of the Committee of the Whole; he votes in case of a tie; he counts and announces votes; he decides in doubtful cases to which standing committees a bill will be assigned; he appoints special or select committees; he appoints the House members to each conference committee; and he maintains decorum in the chamber.[1]

And Fenno makes a wise summary, "Because the procedural controls of the Speaker extend fairly broadly across the stages through which legislative proposals must pass before they emerge as law, the scope of his procedural influence is probably more important than its weight at any one point."[2]

The Senate Majority Leader

There is no true counterpart in the Senate to the Speaker of the House. The very fact that the Senate is only a quarter of the size of the House, and that its members are elected for six years (roughly a third coming up every two years), has a profound influence upon rules and organization. Floor action in the House would be chaotic without tight procedural and presiding officer controls. The House has not enjoyed unlimited debate since the War of 1812. In the Senate, on the other hand, the presiding officer is a figurehead. Most business is conducted by unanimous consent after informal dialogue between the majority and minority leaders.

Insofar as there is a pre-eminent source of power in the Senate, it is in the person of the majority leader. This is especially true when the Democratic party is in control; for the Democrats have given to their majority leader presiding authority over their three most powerful partisan instrumentalities: the Democratic Conference (caucus), the Steering Committee (which makes committee assignments), and the Policy Committee (which controls the scheduling of floor consideration of bills). In the words of Ralph Huitt, the majority leader's power derives from the fact that " . . . he is the center of the Senatorial party's communications network and has access to the President if they are of the same party."[3] He also has a parliamentary edge. He has the right to be recognized first, at his choice, on the floor of the Senate.

Even with these advantages, however, the majority leader's success is based largely upon his personal qualities. Some majority leaders like Alben Barkley and Lyndon Johnson have gained extraordinary power through the exercise of their bargaining, compromising, or manipulating skills. Others like Scott Lucas and Mike Mansfield have been laissez-faire, depending upon the superordinate power of the President and the subordinate party machinery of the whips to produce effective majority rule. One of the regrets of Democratic activists vis-à-vis the Ted Kennedy tragedy in the Summer of 1969 was that it reduced centripetal tendencies within the majority party in the Senate. As majority whip, Kennedy gave promise of filling a power vacuum caused by Mike Mansfield's lack of charismatic leadership. The enigmatic events surrounding the death of Mary Jo Kopechne substantially weakened Kennedy's ability to transform the function of the office of whip from one of simple information-gathering about the voting intentions of members into that of a catalyst of party unity.

Minority Leadership

On the minority side, the picture is more easily drawn. It is clear that the minority leader is the most important minority party official in each House. Like the majority leader, he is supported by whips for floor business. The minority leader is, of course, conditioned by various party conferences and committees which have responsibility for developing party policies and agendas and for assigning party members to standing committees. Republicans have tended to proliferate rather than centralize responsibility for these various partisan instrumentalities. Some minority leaders have operated with great shrewdness and verve. Few have matched the skill of the late Everett Dirksen (R., Illinois).

Committee Assignments

In terms of influencing legislative business and behavior, the two most powerful functions in Congress are, first, control over committee assignments, and second, control over the legislative agenda. Perhaps the most significant shifts in power in the Congress over the past two decades have involved these two functions. The shifts have strengthened the power of party leadership vis-à-vis standing committee chairmen in both cases. This does not mean that the epicenters of party power and committee power are now identical. It does mean that in recent years the overlaps have become quite as observable as the hiatuses. It is therefore possible at this time to classify the majority instruments for the making of committee assignments and for setting the legislative agenda as among the centripetal, party-oriented forces in each house. Even a few years ago, such a classification would have been misleading. The shifts have been clearer in the Senate than in the House, and in the Democratic party than in the Republican; but both chambers and both parties are undergoing a similar transformation.

In the Senate, the Democratic majority leader has very substantial influence in the Steering Committee, which makes committee assignments. Lyndon Johnson used that influence in 1953 to give freshman senators at least one major committee assignment each. This procedure, now known as "the Johnson Rule," has been followed subsequently. It was a departure from an earlier custom that freshman senators were to be assigned to minor committees first (e.g., Post Office and Civil Service, District of Columbia, Government Operations, etc.) and were to be transferred to major committees (e.g., Foreign Relations, Banking and Currency, Armed Services, etc.) only after they had accumulated seniority and had "proved" themselves to the relevant major committee chairmen. Johnson's action through his leadership of the Democratic Steering Committee in modifying the seniority principle was to strengthen the centripetal as against the centrifugal forces in the Democratic party in the Senate. In January 1965 the Republican Committee on Committees adopted a similar principle of modifying seniority as the paramount basis for committee assignments.

Actually, the representative character of the Senate Democratic Steering Committee has been, until recently, bitterly challenged by certain liberal Senators—notably by former Senator Joseph Clark of Pennsylvania.[4] Clark and others were angered by what they considered to be the overrepresentation of southerners and conservatives on a committee that should, they felt, be truly representative of the liberally oriented Democratic majorities across the nation and within the Senate itself. As a result of this liberal protest and of the Democratic landslide of 1964, the Steering Committee was enlarged from fifteen to seventeen members in January 1965. As the decade of the '70's opens, the Democratic Steering Committee in the Senate consists of eight liberals, five moderates, and only four die-hard conservatives. This is simply another example of how traditional structures in Congress adjust ultimately to new forces and pressures from the society generally.

In the House, the Democratic members of the Ways and Means Committee serve as that party's "Committee on Committees." When the Democrats organize the House, the power of the Ways and Means Committee chairman stems not only from the importance of the substantive measures to come before that committee; it stems also from his influence as chairman of the Democratic Committee on Committees. He is then one of the three most powerful men in the House of Representatives, sharing that honor with the Speaker and with the chairman of the Rules Committee.

Procedurally, the Committee on Committees in each house makes its committee recommendations to the Democratic caucus, or, on the Republican side, to the "Conference," which normally ratifies without dissent the recommendations of the committee. The majority leadership works out party ratios on committees with the minority leadership. Finally, caucus or conference action is sanctioned by a *pro forma* floor vote. The House and the Senate are the final legitimators of previous party and interparty decisions.

Control Over the Legislative Agenda

The second most powerful influence on the legislative process, the determination of the legislative agenda, is handled quite differently in the Senate and the House. In the Senate, the schedule of floor business is worked out by the majority leader (occasionally with the advice of a policy committee), always conferring with the minority leadership in order to assure the "unanimous consent" without which the Senate could not manipulate its rules and expedite its business.

In the House, there are a number of calendars. Some of them (Consent Calendar, Calendar Wednesday, District Calendar) are normally used to clear noncontroversial bills. Major bills are registered on the so-called Union Calendar (if raising money is involved) or the House Calendar (if money is not involved). All major bills are sent to the House Rules Committee, except for certain privileged categories of bills (e.g., those emanating from the Appropriations or Ways and Means Committees and some, like "pork barrel," of special interest to constituencies across the nation).

The House Rules Committee

Ever since the truncating of "Uncle Joe" Cannon's powers as speaker in 1910, the Rules Committee has been a separate force in the

House. Arrogating to itself without challenge the right not only to schedule floor debates and amendments for pending bills, but to amend bills in committee, to block them entirely, and even to report out legislation *de novo,* the Rules Committee became for a generation a House within a House. From 1937 to the early 1960's, it served as a major vehicle for emasculating or blocking "liberal" legislation, even when the President and a majority of the House favored such bills. Some of the measures that disappeared in the Rules Committee graveyard during these thirty years involved civil rights, health insurance, housing, wage legislation, and federal aid to education. Republican as well as Democratic Presidents found their majority leadership unable to break the stranglehold of the dominant coalition in the Rules Committee. It is not without reason that Representative Bolling referred to the House Rules Committee as an "efficiently run legislative cemetery."[5]

That is why the 1961 fight by President Kennedy, with the help of Speaker Sam Rayburn, to enlarge the Rules Committee by adding two additional liberal members was such an important milestone in the history of the House. Enlarging the Rules Committee was the only way to make it at all responsive to majority leadership, since at that time it was strategically impossible to change the rules themselves. Even so, Kennedy did not get everything he wanted. His "safe" majority on the Rules Committee turned out not to be "safe" on federal aid to education. But the 1961 struggle broke the tight control of the inverted coalition. In 1965 the power of the majority party in Rules Committee deliberations was further strengthened by two new House rules.[6] The first, the 21-Day Rule, gave to the Speaker the right to recognize a committee chairman or other member of a standing committee for the purpose of allowing a majority vote to force the Rules Committee to report out a particular bill it had been considering for twenty-one days or more. The second rule gave the Speaker the right to offer a motion sending a bill to Conference Committee by majority vote, thereby precluding the power of the Rules Committee to block assignment of bills to Conference.

The 21-day Rule was revoked by the 90th Congress in 1967, but by then it had become largely superfluous. For in that same year, as a condition of his accession the chairmanship of the Rules Committee, Representative William Colmer (Mississippi) promised to support a liberalizing set of rules to govern the Committee's procedures. These new rules took from the chairman the right to set meeting dates—a power used by a former chairman, Howard Smith (Virginia), to delay or block action on liberal legislation. The new rules also required majority consent before a bill could be tabled by the chairman, and they set limits on proxy voting by members.

The long and short of it is that the Rules Committee, until recently the major bastion of conservative power in the House, is now a largely benign gatekeeper. It is doubtful that ever again will it be allowed to become a consistent instrument of minority prejudice.

Campaign and Patronage Committees

Any description of the formal machinery of "party" would be incomplete without reference to the party campaign committees in the Senate and the House.

The campaign committees had their origins in the immediate post-Civil War period when "almost unbearable strains developed between President Andrew Johnson and the so-called radicals who dominated the Republican party in Congress during his term of office. For fear that President Johnson would use the power of the national party to help crush re-election hopes, the radicals organized their own campaign committee to assist them in the 1866 election."[7]

Today both parties in both houses have such committees. Until recently, the relationship of these congressional campaign committees to their respective national committees was awkward, if not downright unfriendly. At the very least, the national committees have been almost totally preoccupied with presidential elections. But another sign of the revolution of the past decade is to be found in the growing cooperation between national committees and the respective congressional campaign committees. Today they share money and research activities, and attempt to dovetail their respective programs during election years. The amount of money that the campaign committees have been able to distribute to party candidates has been small compared to other sources of income. But the monetary value of other services provided by the committee (advertising boiler plate, radio and television tapes, voting records, speech kits, etc.) is not inconsiderable. As the national committees, with their enormous fund-raising potentials, become more closely related to congressional campaign committees, another link will be forged between the presidential and congressional wings of each party, strengthening centripetal tendencies in national politics.

The System in Transition

The basic shifts that have occurred in the organization and party leadership of both houses in the past decade have taken place, of course, by "tipping scales," not by explosive inversions of power. One may still refer, therefore, to the congressional system as procedurally conservative while acknowledging the increased liberality of its output.

Here we turn from formal organization in the Congress to informal influence. Richard Fenno refers to the progressions of power for new members of the House as the "seniority-protégé-apprenticeship" system. We shall review the seniority issue in the next chapter. It is sufficient here to note that length of service is an important ingredient, even a requisite, of power in most organizations. The principle has been virtually reified in the United States Congress, although important exceptions presently exist. Even the exceptions, however, are generally granted by those who already are secure in their seniority (e.g., the appointment of a subcommittee chairman on other than seniority grounds by a committee chairman who has long held seniority).

The "seniority-protégé-apprenticeship" system has in the past generation been a virtually unchallenged pattern of personal advancement, at least in the House of Representatives. Lines in what William White has called the "inner club" in the Senate have been more subtle. However, length of service is still of substantial significance in the arrogation of power in both houses.

There is no simple, positive correlation between seniority and party loyalty as measured by roll call votes on important presidential bills. In fact, some of the key guardians of congressional bastions of power and influence have seen too many Presidents and legislative party leaders come and go to be sensitive to their pleas or threats.

How then do those loyal to *party* get ahead? Why pay attention to centripetal rather than centrifugal forces in the Congress? To put the matter cynically, "what is there in it for me"—in personal advancement in the power structure of the House or Senate—to pay attention to party leadership instead of deferring to the wishes of those who have seniority in the traditional committee system?

Until recently, the answer was "very little." The rule has been, within the Democratic party at least, that those who have voted the party line as structured by the President and at the same time have attempted to strengthen the centripetal influences of party in each house have been rewarded with a kind of refined "Coventry." Senators like Proxmire and McCarthy; representatives like Bolling and Reuss come to mind. Party leaders have been found not among the defenders of party, but among potential brokers between the traditionally hostile forces of party and seniority. Since conservative forces have dominated such key committees as Democratic Policy and Democratic Steering in the Senate, and Ways and Means and Rules in the House (to say nothing of a majority of standing committees in both houses), it seemed clear that if one was to "get along" one would have to "go along."

But suppose today that one is a freshman representative or senator in the majority party and sees:

——the enlargement and liberalization of party policy and steering committees in the Senate;
——the shift in power from the Rules Committee to the Speaker in the House;
——the improved and institutionalized liaison between the White House and the Congress;

——the increasingly close relationships between the national committees and the campaign committees;

——the massive registration of Blacks in the South (pursuant to the Civil Rights Act of 1965) and its probable effect upon southern conservatives who presently dominate a number of committees, and most of whom in any case are old men;

——the shifts of power in certain committees because of the death or retirement of conservative southern chairmen;

——the long-range effects of reapportionment upon both external and internal congressional expectations.

Would not this array of developments modify one's desire to support traditional committee power against the forces of President or congressional party leadership? The fact is that "getting ahead" within the system involves a different calculus than it did a few years back.

It will, of course, take time for the Democrats, especially in the House, to get used to these new tendencies and developments. The members have operated for so many years on the basis of conditioned reflexes, salivating to southern accents, that the more cosmopolitan and urbanized accents of party leadership still sound strange and confusing.

In any case, while centripetal tendencies phase in, the echoes of ancient wars will continue to clash in the corridors and cloakrooms. State delegations will continue to caucus on behalf of their cherished particularisms; small bands of the like-minded (Acorns, Marching and Chowder Society, etc.) will continue to "meat" and drink and talk; regional organizations like Omar Burleson's Southern Democrats will plot both regional and ideological strategy; the Democratic Study Group of party- and presidentially-oriented liberal Democrats will continue to press the leadership against "unwarranted" concessions to southern "Bourbons." And, of course, the standing committees and subcommittees will continue their stratagems for autonomy and segmented power. In some areas, as we shall see, these atomistic forces will continue to get their way.

But it will never again be the same. The nationalizing forces—the centripetal forces—have tipped the balance inexorably. The Republican party is as subject to these long-range developments as the Democrats. The Nixon victory in 1969 is bound over time to give the Republicans in Congress a new sense of mission and party purpose. As this sense develops, a new and tighter leadership and a new integration of disparate Republican leadership organizations will emerge in both houses, paralleling the developments on "the other side of the aisle."

Chapter V

CENTRIFUGAL FORCES: COMMITTEES AND SENIORITY

The argument up to this point has been that secular shifts in the society and in the base of congressional power are producing changes in the nature of the congressional system. The essential change is found in the increase in the power and influence of the President and of the party leadership in both houses at the expense of committee chairmen and of their supporting interests.

In this chapter we reflect that the traditional committee system in Congress still has considerable autonomy and power, and that the precise way of describing the new Congress must be in terms of a point on a spectrum. Rule by committee chairmen, chosen by seniority and sensitive to the exogenous inputs of particular constituencies and special interests, stands at one end of the spectrum; rule by party leaders, sensitive especially to the exogenous inputs of the President, stands at the other. Congress in the early 1970's occupies roughly a middle position between these two extremes. What is revolutionary is that for most of the past three generations, Congress has occupied a position on the spectrum close to the "seniority-committee" end.

The Role of Committees

Every year, especially during spring vacation, tourists haunt the galleries of the two houses of Congress looking for democracy at work. Many of these visitors are shocked and disillusioned. If the House is in session, the chances are overwhelming that its proceedings will seem to the casual visitor listless, highly structured, and deadly dull. The Senate may be effectively empty: the majority and minority leaders perhaps in their places in the front seats on either side of the aisle; a few senators reading newspapers, not paying any attention to the lawmaker who at the moment holds the floor. The only person hanging on every word is the court stenographer whose function it is to spend his days recording and transcribing for the *Congressional Record* the floor remarks of our national legislators.

The fact is that Congress at work is Congress in committee. It is inconceivable that Congress could perform its various functions without a committee system. There are of course many kinds of committees. Some of them, especially those related to party organization, we have already met. In addition, there are joint committees made up of members from both the Senate and the House. Joint committees are generally more concerned with investigations, research, and surveillance than with legislation (e.g., Joint Economic Committee, Joint Committee on Internal Revenue Taxation, Joint Committee on Reduction of Nonessential Federal Expenditures). The Joint Committee on Atomic Energy is in a class by itself. Its powers over the Atomic Energy Commission are so substantial as to raise at least theoretical questions about what appears to be a massive and unconstitutional invasion of executive branch prerogatives.

Conference Committees

Then, of course, there are conference committees. Conference committees must, in the tension between centripetal and centrifugal tendencies in the Congress, be considered neuters. Appointed ad hoc by party leaders in each house, members sent to conference are in fact generally selected by the chairman and ranking minority members of the relevant standing committees. The selection is normally based on considerations of seniority. The job of conference committees is, of course, to resolve differences between House and Senate versions of a particular bill. Although conference committees have been criticized on occasion for acting as a third house of Congress, scholarly evidence seems to indicate that they have seldom abused their positions, and have in fact performed with remarkable astuteness the difficult and essential task of compromising interhouse differences.[1] On occasion, the President exerts pressure on conferees—especially to delete embarrassing restrictions on his discretion in foreign affairs. But in general conference committees are neither instruments of the President and party nor instruments of committee chairmen and other centrifugal forces in the Congress. They are what they pretend to be: instruments of interhouse negotiation and compromise.

Select and special committees we shall ignore, except to note that they are ad hoc, largely investigative, and rarely report out legislation.

Standing Committees

The bulk of congressional work is performed by standing committees—that is, committees with stated jurisdictions, created by the rules in each house, permanent (at least until the rules are changed), and responsible for screening, examining, and reporting on legislation or other business referred to them. The standing committees have been created over time in response to pressing national problems. The evolution of committees on Public Lands, Agriculture, Insular Affairs, Banking and Currency, Education and Labor, Atomic Energy, Armed Services, and Science and Astronautics have been symbolic of major developments in the historic concerns of the American people.

Perhaps the most important thing to be said about congressional standing committees is that they are uneven in prestige. The greater importance of some committees over others has given to those who control or influence committee assignments a powerful weapon to induce cooperation from more junior legislators. One political scientist who has studied Congress closely, H. Douglas Price, has given an intuitive ranking to the committees as follows:

Standing Committees (ranked in groups, by order of importance)

Senate	House
I	I
Appropriations	Rules
Foreign Relations	Appropriations
Finance	Ways and Means
II	II
Armed Services	Armed Services
Judiciary	Judiciary
Agriculture & Forestry	Agriculture
Interstate & Foreign Commerce	Interstate & Foreign Commerce
	Foreign Affairs
	Government Operations

III	III
Banking & Currency	Banking & Currency
Labor & Public Welfare	Education & Labor
Public Works	Interior & Insular Affairs
Interior & Insular Affairs	Science & Astronautics
Aeronautical & Space Sciences	Public Works
IV	IV
Post Office & Civil Service	Post Office & Civil Service
Government Operations	Merchant Marine & Fisheries
	Veterans Affairs
	Internal Security
V	V
District of Columbia	District of Columbia
Rules & Administration	House Administration

Before both sessions of any Congress are over, these thirty-six committees will have disposed of nearly twenty thousand bills (mostly by pigeonholing); they will have held hundreds of hearings on major legislation; they will have met in innumerable executive sessions (closed to the press and public) to work out improvements and compromises in legislative language and in the wording of committee reports. Some of the committees in the Senate will have passed upon several thousand military, foreign service, or top political executive appointments submitted by the President under the constitutional provisions for "advice and consent." And finally, in both houses, hundreds of private bills will have been reported out for favorable action on the floor, usually by unanimous consent. (Private bills are bills dealing with individual matters, such as immigration and naturalization cases, claims against the government, land titles, etc.)

Congressional standing committees exist to speed the work load; to facilitate meaningful deliberations on important measures and issues; to develop a degree of expertise among committee members and committee staff; and to serve as a convenient graveyard for inept proposals. They constitute the great baronies of congressional power. Many of them look outward in jealous competition with the President, with their opposite committee in the other house, and with the whole house of which they are a part. When internally unified and buttressed in parliamentary privilege by special rules, as in the case of the House Appropriations Committee, they can almost at will dominate the business of the parent chamber.[2]

The Growth of Subcommittees

Prior to the Legislative Reorganization Act of 1946, Congress had almost twice the number of committees it presently has. The consolidation of committee structure in 1946 was, however, soon followed by a proliferation of subcommittees. Today, Capitol Hill boasts nearly two hundred and fifty subcommittees. A couple of examples, one from each house, indicates typical subcommittee structure:

SENATE

COMMITTEE ON FOREIGN RELATIONS

Subcommittees:
- African Affairs
- Economic and Social Policy Affairs
- European Affairs
- Far Eastern Affairs
- International Organization and Disarmament Affairs
- Near Eastern and South Asian Affairs
- Ocean Space
- U.S. Security Agreements and Commitments Abroad
- Western Hemisphere Affairs

HOUSE

COMMITTEE ON APPROPRIATIONS

Subcommittees:
- Agriculture
- Defense
- District of Columbia
- Foreign Operations
- Independent Offices
- Interior and Related Agencies
- Labor, Health, Education & Welfare
- Legislative
- Military Construction
- Public Works
- State, Justice, Commerce and Judiciary
- Transportation
- Treasury, Post Office, and Executive Office.

In consequence of the growth of subcommittees, a senator may find himself on only two committees, but on seven to ten subcommittees. A member of the House, limited to one committee assignment, may find himself on anywhere from two to six subcommittees.

Subcommittees are quite as necessary as committees. They are the congressional response to the weight and complexity of the agenda of legislative business. They represent the ultimate division of labor in congressional organization above the level of the individual legislator. They also give a wide opportunity for able and hardworking legislators to earn early recognition and experience in the fundamental work of Congress.

But there are also penalities paid for the proliferation of subcommittees. First, because one subcommittee tends to defer to another, subcommittee consideration may be tantamount to full committee consideration, which in turn may be tantamount to full house and even congressional consideration. This deference puts an inordinate amount of power in the hands of strategically placed subcommittee chairmen and members. Second, what subcommittees gain in expertise may be offset by the parochialisms and prejudices that their specialization has either created or exacerbated among their membership. Third, although the system of mutual deference which subcommittees inevitably promote may improve civility and interpersonal cohesion in the Congress, it can also produce a massive logrolling operation ("you scratch my back and I'll scratch yours"), which can be the effective enemy of rational public interest considerations. But subcommittees are unquestionably here to stay, and in a perverse way they may strengthen presidential rather than committee-chairmen power in the Congress. Committee chairmen may defer to their subcommittees to the point of ignoring what they are up to; Presidents cannot afford this luxury. With the institutionalization of presidential interest in the fate of his legislation, a President may be far more acutely aware of what is happening in the subcommittee than is the full-committee chairman. Furthermore, a subcommittee chairman or member may get far more ego satisfaction (and ultimate political benefit) from being cultivated by the President or top White House staff than from his relations with his full-committee chairman.

This reality has set up tensions more than once between full-committee chairmen and subcommittee chairmen. The successful subcommittee chairman is one who can refrain from antagonizing the full-committee chairman who appointed him, at the same time that he maintains enough autonomy to be cultivated directly by other congressmen, by constituents or group interests, and by the President. This may seem to be a difficult tight rope, but walking this kind of wire successfully is the adroit politician's stock in trade.

Seniority

Although seniority has been tempered by several recent changes, it is still one of the most potent centrifugal forces in Congress. Seniority, when tied to a high degree of division of labor and mutual deference, unquestionably places extraordinary power in the hands of a few men. It shapes patterns of advancement within the two houses. It sets up toll gates not only for the casual legislative wayfarer, but for speakers, majority leaders, and even Presidents. If committees are frequently attacked, in the words of the *Congressional Quarterly*, as "bastions of conservatism, obstructive units subject to control by special interests, and dictatorships ruled by misfits,"[3] it is because old men from "safe" and rurally dominated states and districts have for years held effective power through seniority.

The full effect of the seniority principle is now felt chiefly at the level of standing committee chairmanships and throughout the structure of the House Appropriations Committee complex. Standing committee chairmen control subcommittee appointments and jurisdictions; they appoint and control most committee staffs; at their pleasure, they represent the committee on the floor and in conference; they usually control committee agendas and committee hearings; they work with other old-timers to form an "inner club" of influence, at least on key committees. The closer one gets to control positions in the major committees (partisan, procedural, and substantive), the surer it is that he has not antagonized the key old-timers who presently occupy major committee chairmanships.

Seniority is often linked in the public mind with conservative southern domination. It is true that in some committees control by conservative southerners is real and is arranged in depth. In fact, if one wishes to rank committes in order of their importance to traditional wielders of power, he need only note the depth of southern appointments. Take, for example, the order of succession on the Democratic side to the House Appropriations Committee as of 1970: George H. Mahon of Texas was chairman; out of the top nine in line of succession, six were from the South. W.R. Poage of Texas was chairman of the Agricultural Committee of the House; the next six in line were *all* from the South. The District of Columbia Committee is not considered an important committee—*except* to those southerners who fear Black control of the government of the nation's capital. In 1970, John L. McMillan of South Carolina was chairman; four out of the six of the next in line came from south of the Mason-Dixon line.In the Senate, southern seniority and succession is most marked on the following committees: Agriculture and Forestry, Armed Services, Appropriations, Finance, and Judiciary. The last named, of course, has jurisdiction over civil rights legislation.

Conservative regional powers are on the wane, however. The fact is that a number of committees are not chaired by conservative southerners, or if they are they have a *non*-southerner or a liberal southerner as ranking majority member (i.e., next in line of succession on the Democratic side). As noted in the Preface, as the decade of the 1970's begins, of the ten Democratic Senators with the greatest seniority, nine come from south of the Mason-Dixon line. Most of these are men in their seventies or older. Of the next ten in terms of seniority only two come from the American South. And it might be noted in addition that, in 1970, of the twenty-one House Committees, fourteen were chaired by representatives from south of the Mason-Dixon line. If power should suddenly pass to the ranking majority member on each committee, the number fourteen would drop to eleven.

Actually, to the President and to party leaders, perhaps the most worrisome concentration of southern seniority has been in the subcommittees of the House Appropriations Committee. Of the twelve subcommittees in 1970, the southerners held (through subcommittee chairmanship) the purse strings on Agriculture; Defense; District of Columbia; Foreign Operations; Independent Offices; Legislative; Military Construction; and Treasury, Post Office, and Executive Office. To this list must be added the chairman of the subcommittee on State, Justice, Commerce, and the Judiciary, Rep. John J. Rooney. Although a Democrat from New York, Mr. Rooney has been strangely parochial and extremely conservative on State Department appropriations. His influence is perhaps compensated for by the liberal leanings of one or two southern subcommittee chairmen.

Even where standing committees are chaired by men of long seniority, the arbitrariness of power and influence has recently been tempered by decisions on the part of some committee majorities to establish curbs upon the powers of their chairmen. And as we noted in the previous chapter, majority and minority leaders in both houses (in other words, the wielders of party power) are chosen on other grounds than seniority (except in the sense that the position of whip may lead to special advantages in being considered for majority leader and then, in the case of the House, Speaker). Subcommittee chairmen are now chosen with only one eye on seniority. The Johnson rule, adopted in principle by both parties, gives a major committee assignment to all freshman senators. Even in the House, attention is frequently given to a man's background in judging to what committees he should be assigned as a freshman. For example, Ambassador Chester Bowles was assigned as a freshman congressman in 1958 to the coveted Foreign Affairs Committee. Such factors as these lead many astute observers of Congress to believe that the answer to seniority is not to end it but to box it.

One generalization that seems to hold up in the study of politics is that few persons give up power willingly. If external expectations and internal functional relations begin to threaten the traditional power of those holding seniority, their reaction is to temper and adjust—preserving the forms of power even while losing some of the reality. This is what is presently happening in the Congress, although this is not to suggest that committee chairmen are simply shadows of their former selves. Relative to President and party leadership, their powers have diminished; but in certain fields of policy (e.g., agriculture, oil, taxation, the domestic implications of defense) their influence is still enormous. And for the ambitious legislator who wishes to get ahead in the influence structure of the congressional system, appropriate deference to the chairmen and ranking majority and minority members of standing committees is still the path of prudence.

When all is said and done, seniority looms large as a factor in congressional behavior, and establishes autonomous centers of power that can be powerful determinants of the fate of policies and of subordinate congressional careers.

Defenders of the seniority system contend that it virtually insures procedural and substantive expertise at the point where 90 percent of the legislative business of Congress takes place; that the automatic feature of seniority saves Congress from the endless wrangles and bitter personal animosities that always surround matters of succession to power in political systems; and that the worst abuses of seniority can be tempered by majoritarian forces within committees and within each house.

It is certainly true that the chairmanships of the some three hundred committee units in the Congress constitute a rich and highly dispersed system of rewards to individual legislators. Without some degree of real (i.e., autonomous) power, these rewards would be hollow. One of the effects of total control of congressional business by President or party would be to make subordinate positions in the congressional system perfunctory, with a probable loss in energy and activity at the committee and subcommittee level. For those who wish to press for a further diminution of the power of chairmen of committees and subcommittees, the question is posed: what, psychologically, would replace the sense of status and deference which autonomous power presently provides not for one or two but for scores of legislators in each house? And can the advantages of a vital and independent legislature be assured without such highly dispersed personal rewards? The answer is by no means clear.

Committee Jurisdictions

The committee components that constitute a major element in the congressional system are plagued by jurisdictional problems. In the earliest Congresses this was no issue, for there were no standing committees. Special or select (ad hoc) committees were created to review particular legislative issues. A committee was dissolved as soon as it reported.

By the 1880's, however, standing committees had become so entrenched as to warrant Woodrow Wilson's comment that Congress, and for that matter the U.S. government, was in fact run by the chairmen of the standing committees.

In 1946 the Legislative Reorganization Act attempted to define committee jurisdictions as unambiguously as possible, and to build a committee's purpose around a major function of the federal government. The problem was not solved, nor has it been solved in the executive branch. A few illustrations will suffice.

The Committee on Foreign Relations in the Senate is commissioned by Senate rules to consider "Relations of the United States with foreign nations generally." And yet, questions of foreign and international relations are considered by at least nine other major committees of the Senate: Aeronautical and Space Sciences; Agriculture and Forestry (e.g., on surplus food disposal); Appropriations; Armed Services; Banking and Currency (on certain international monetary questions); Commerce; Finance (on trade and tariff legislation); Judiciary (on immigration and refugee policy); Government Operations (especially the subcommittee on National Security and International Operations).

In the House, a similar overlap occurs.

The same kinds of jurisdictional questions affect domestic legislation. And how does one distinguish any longer between domestic and foreign questions? In 1962 the Communications Satellite Bill was referred to two Senate committees, first Commerce and then Foreign Relations.

One interesting logic of jurisdictional ambiguities in the committee system is the upgrading of the discretion of party leaders in assigning bills to committee. More than one bill has been helped by the President pro tem or the Speaker assigning it to a "favorable" rather than an "unfavorable" committee.

These substantive confusions are, of course, in addition to the continuing question of the appropriate relationship between *legislative* committees and the *appropriations* committees. Legislative committees are allowed to *authorize* expenditures to carry out certain legislative purposes. But the Treasury of the United States cannot, except through what is called "backdoor financing," pay anyone a dime for anything unless an *authorization* has been legitimated and made precise by an *appropriation.* Since money bills, constitutionally, must originate in the House, the House Appropriations Committee and its subcommittees become powerful jurisdictional rivals of most of the legislative committees. To a lesser extent, the rivalry exists in the Senate, mitigated in part by the practice of legislative committee representatives of attending appropriations committee deliberations.

The congressional system has adjusted to some of the jurisdictional problems of its committees: joint hearings sometimes occur; a few standing joint committees have been established (notably Atomic Energy, Defense Production, Economic Committee, and Internal Revenue Taxation); committee staff collaborations occasionally occur. But overlaps and hiatuses are frequent. No complete answer is possible in the legislative branch any more than it is in the executive branch. Actually, the very ambiguity of committee jurisdiction tends to increase the power of party leaders in both houses, for ambiguity implies discretion in referring bills to committee. Nevertheless, the problem of committee jurisdiction needs at least intermittent attention by congressional reformers with a penchant for tidiness and updatedness. Archaic committee jurisdictions can, among other things, preclude needed executive branch reorganization.

Committee Staffs

The centrifugal tendencies of seniority and of the division of congressional labor among committees and subcommittees are frequently exacerbated by committee staffs. The Legislative Reorganization Act of 1946 provided for additional staff assistance to individual senators and congressmen and for a greatly extended Legislative Reference Service in the Library of Congress. It also established an authorization for professionally qualified staffs to the various standing committees of Congress. Up to four staff members and up to six clerks were provided for each committee. A larger number of both staff members and clerks were specified for certain "busy" committees, like Appropriations.

The hope was that committee staffs would reduce the reliance of Congress upon executive and pressure group expertise, giving Congress in essence its own substantive experts—an independent source of information. It was also hoped that professional staffs would help to screen out poorly drawn or silly bills, enabling the legislators to concentrate more fully and systematically upon a lightened agenda. Neither hope has been realized. By and large, committee staff appointments have not been qualitatively equal to the expertise in the executive branch or in many lobby headquarters. In addition, congressional staff must cover a far wider variety of problems than their executive branch or pressure-group counterparts. The extent of congressional dependence on outside sources of information and analysis is still high. Furthermore, committee staffs have helped proliferate the very business they were supposed to limit. In the two years following the Legislative Reorganization Act of 1946, the volume of bills introduced in Congress nearly doubled, and it has continued high ever since. Who can doubt that the increase in this aspect of congressional business was due in part to the creation of additional staff, personal and committee?

This is not to question for a moment the importance of staff services to the standing committees, or the high degree of professional competence of many staff directors and assistants. It is to suggest that the record is uneven in terms of the legislative intent of the Legislative Reorganization Act. It is further to suggest that committee staffs, most of them appointed by and loyal to the chairmen are "knights to the barons" not "knights to the king,"—if by "king" we mean the President and party.

Staff members as well as legislators can develop a touchy sense of jurisdictional interest, and frequently they educate their superiors to positions of intransigence and jealously which their superiors would not have had the time or inclination to develop on their own. More than one legislator has had to quiet the tempers, or come to the rescue, of committee staffs "threatened" by another committee staff or by some real or imagined manifestation of executive branch hubris. The proliferation of staff has inevitably turned many congressmen and senators into managers as well as legislators, and has consequently skewed their attention to problems of internal conflict resolution within their several fiefdoms. Whether this represents a net gain for congressional efficiency and deliberation is doubtful.

The minority party in the Congress feels shortchanged in staff services on many committees. This inequity should obviously be redressed, but it is by no means certain that the best interests of the Congress or the nation are served by a further general proliferation of committee staff. Paul Appleby once remarked that those who would make Congress more expert are the most truly subversive of representative government. What he had in mind, of course, were hearings (such as some of those conducted by the Joint Committee on Atomic Energy) in which highly specialized committee staff ask questions of scientists from executive departments and agencies. Neither the congressmen (if, in truth, any are present) nor the general public can possibly have the foggiest notion of what such hearings are all about. Dean Acheson suggests that what congressmen need is not "larger staffs and extensive organizations," but "time to inform themselves and to think."[4]

Sub-Governments

The ultimate centrifugal force in the congressional system, and in the entire federal government, is the three-way partnership sometimes found among congressional committees (or chairmen of subcommittees), powerful bureaus in federal departments or agencies, and well-organized outside pressure groups. This partnership, at its most efficient, creates what Douglass Cater has called "sub-governments."[5]

Cater sees the greatest concentration of sub-governments in the field of defense. Secretaries of Defense, with the full backing of Presidents, have made heroic efforts to impose national-interest, cost-benefit standards upon military procurement and organization. Congress has, however, repeatedly followed the lead of its constituent committees and subcommittees in defeating such attempts. Armed Services Committees and Appropriations subcommittees, with informal linkages to the three military services and to their private counterparts and suppliers (Navy League, Association of the U.S. Army, Aerospace Industries Association, etc.), develop their own independent sense of what the nation needs. The power of sub-governments in the defense field is directly related to the ubiquity of the impact of defense spending. All states and almost all congressional districts are affected by Pentagon decisions—decisions about opening or closing bases, making or canceling hardware contracts, disposing of surplus property, or changing military organization and pay. In an otherwise glowing relationship with the first session of the 89th Congress, President Johnson met resounding defeat, delays tantamount to defeat, or humiliating revisions at the hands of Congress on a number of issues affecting the Pentagon. A proposed National Guard-Reserve merger was blocked; the military pay bill was raised to almost double that requested by the President; and the Secretary's right to close bases was hedged about with delays and congressional committee clearances—restrictions which were mild compared to those previously vetoed by the President. Perhaps in no other area of public policy do the exogenous inputs of constituences and group interests more effectively and insidiously overshadow presidential and party influences on congressional behavior.

There are, however, some close seconds. Oil comes to mind, with its almost sacrosanct depletion allowances for tax purposes; so does the "pork barrel" triumvirate of the Army Corps of Engineers, the Public Works Committees of Congress, and the National Rivers and Harbors Congress; so do sections of agriculture, with their defenders in the bureaus and desks of the Department of Agriculture, the Agricultural Committees and Appropriations subcommittees of the Congress, and powerful commodity lobbies on the outside.

As noted in Chapter II, sub-governments are far from constituting the major congeries of power in Washington. But it is one of the facts of political life that some sub-governments are extremely powerful—so powerful, in fact, that President and party have little chance of controlling them. The basic presidential and party strategy then becomes one of bargaining public interest legislation against special interest legislation, hopefully getting as much of the former for as little of the latter as possible.

Committee chairmen, subcommittee chairmen, seniority, committee staffs, and sub-governments can, under certain circumstances, all be friends of party and President. But under other circumstances, they can be divisive, separatist, autonomous centers of centrifugal force, responsive to special interests and unfriendly to presidential or party influence.

Whatever the increase in presidential and party power in the legislative process, centrifugal influences will continue to be an important element in the congressional system. They may in part represent special privilege and lumpiness of advantage; but in a perverse way, they may also represent the precondition of maintaining in Congress a healthy independence from executive domination. In the last analysis Congress can have no power if congressmen and committees have no power.

To this general issue we will return in the final chapter.

Chapter *VI*

THE DYNAMICS OF THE CENTRIPETAL SYSTEM: A DECADE AND A HALF OF CIVIL RIGHTS LEGISLATION

The proof of changes in the environment of the congressional system and of functional relations within it is found in the nature of the system's output. In the fifteen years 1956-1970 no congeries of legislative issues more dramatically registered shifts in epicenters of power in the Congress, or secular shifts in national attitudes about matters of importance, than major measures in the field of civil rights. The struggles over civil rights legislation highlight both the growing strength of the centripetal system and, more recently, the growing influence of a tax-conscious, economically and socially insecure, lower middle class in the American political system generally.

Essentially, the period from 1956 to 1968 witnessed the end of the power of a militant southern minority to block or seriously emasculate civil rights legislation aimed at the protection of America's Black minority. It saw a shift in the appraisals of presidential and congressional party leadership about the urgency of federal action and about the possibilities of breaking the obstructive power of the inverted coalition in both the Senate and the House. It saw an increase in both substantive and procedural toughness on civil rights questions: the bills became increasingly strong and extensive in their attacks upon discrimination; presidential and party leadership became increasingly committed to the use of procedural power to overcome southern opposition. The culmination of the drive was the Civil Rights Act of 1968.

From 1966 on, however, as manifestations of Black militancy increased in the ghettos of the great cities of the North and West; as welfare costs and urban crime continued to soar; as student activists (Black and white) turned universities, colleges, and high schools into battlefields; as the Vietnam war kept taxes high; and as inflation eroded the economic gains of factory workers and the urban middle class generally; the pressure for further congressional action in the field of civil rights (as in other fields of reform) was partially countered by constituent demands to "slow down." By late 1969, when Dr. George Gallup asked the question, "What is your opinion—do you think that the racial integration of schools in the United States is going too fast or not fast enough?"—44% of the respondents answered "too fast." Only 22% answered "not fast enough." The other 34% answered "about right" (25%) or "no opinion" (9%).[1]

During a fifteen-year period, then, the power of the South over civil rights issues was broken by a national majority will as interpreted by presidents and congressional party leaders. But toward the end of this period, the majority will itself had begun to shift. Ten million votes for George Wallace, and the victory of Richard Nixon, in 1968 were, in part, barometers of new anxieties in American life that far transcended the sullen war in Southeast Asia.

1956-1965: A DECADE OF PROCEDURAL REFORMS AND SUBSTANTIVE VICTORIES

Prior to 1956, civil rights bills were regularly aborted by referral to the hostile Judiciary Committee in the Senate and by pigeonholing actions of the equally hostile Rules Committee in the House. By 1965 these and other forces of obstruction in committee and on the floor had been overcome by a benign coalition responding to presidential pressure and to bipartisan leadership in both houses. As a result of these shifts in power, civil rights legislation moved in a single decade from ineffectual piety, through concern with investigating the problem and positing effectively unenforceable voting rights, to the establishment of new and broad definitions of nondiscrimination in employment and public accommodations, and finally to the creation of unambiguous machinery for direct federal intervention in securing for the Blacks the right to vote. Congress also approved the use of administrative discretion in cutting off federal funds from programs where discrimination is encountered, as in the field of education.

We now turn to the details of the procedural changes which made these substantive victories possible.

There are at least five hurdles which bills must negotiate in the Congress between introduction and passage. Proponents must negotiate all five; antagonists need only block once. This is why defensive strength is generally more powerful than offensive strength in the legislative process. The five hurdles are: (1) the legislative committee stage in the Senate; (2) the floor stage in the Senate; (3) the legislative committee stage in the House; (4) the Rules Committee stage in the House; and (5) the floor stage in the House. Additional barriers may, of course, be established in the Appropriations Committees of both houses and in conference committees. But no one has to worry about funding or about interhouse agreements if basic legislation has been previously thwarted in either house. A successful negotiation of the five basic procedural hurdles is therefore vital. For proponents of civil rights legislation, the barriers in the Senate had proved insurmountable prior to 1957.

Senate Committee Stage—Overpowering the Judiciary Committee

In the Senate most civil rights legislation has traditionally fallen under the jurisdiction of the Senate Judiciary Committee. Chaired for decades by conservatives, mostly southern, the Judiciary Committee has in the past constituted the first defensive line of anti-civil rights forces in the upper chamber. Note, for example, the treatment accorded President Eisenhower's first civil rights offering.

1956

In early 1956 Eisenhower sent to the Hill a measure which, among other things, created a Civil Rights Commission and conferred authority on the attorney general to initiate suits for the protection of civil rights. The bill in the Senate had been assigned to the Judiciary Committee, whose chairman was Senator James O. Eastland, segregationist Democrat from Mississippi. Although a subcommittee had held hearings and approved four measures, the full Judiciary Committee never reported the bills to the floor. Later, when a companion measure was passed by the House and delivered to the Senate floor, the bill was given its first and second readings under unanimous consent while senators favoring the bill were absent from the floor, and was also referred to the fatal embrace of the Judiciary Committee.

Pro-civil rights forces then made an attempt to file a discharge petition, a device which, if adopted, would have forced the Judiciary Committee to send the bill to the floor. But the majority leader, Lyndon

Johnson, operating in those years from conservative premises procedurally and substantively, stymied the request by calling for an overnight recess. The next morning, when the attempt to present the petition was renewed, the chair ruled it out of order except by unanimous consent, on the grounds that since the Senate had recessed and not adjourned, it was still the same legislative day as it had been the day before and therefore no Morning Hour would be held for the introduction of bills and petitions. A few days later the 84th Congress ended, without the backers of the civil rights bill having even gotten action on their petition.

1957

The following year the story began in much the same way. President Eisenhower requested a measure similar to the one rejected in 1956. Introduced in both the Senate and the House, it asked for a Civil Rights Commission to investigate problems and recommend solutions; an additional assistant attorney general to head a Civil Rights Division in the Justice Department; new legal protections for the right to vote; and perhaps most important, authorization for the attorney general to initiate suits to seek injunctions against deprivation of any civil rights. This last provision, Title III in the bill, was the most disliked by its opponents, for it raised the specter of the federal government initiating school and public facility desegregation cases throughout the South.

In the Senate the bill was referred to Senator Eastland's Judiciary Committee, but the subcommittee to which it was assigned for initial review was chaired by Senator Thomas Hennings of Missouri, an ardent proponent of civil rights legislation. The following account by Howard E. Schuman shows how the committee process, in the hands of a chairman unfriendly to civil rights, can be used for mortal purposes:

> A number of civil rights bills were introduced during the first days of the session. On January 22, Senator Hennings moved in committee that February 18 be set as the deadline for ending hearings on them and that a vote on the legislation and the reporting of a bill to the Senate should not be delayed beyond one further week. This motion was not acted on.
>
> Four days later on January 26 the 14 bills by then in committee were referred to the Constitutional Rights Subcommittee.
>
> On January 30 Senator Hennings, the chairman, presented an omnibus bill to the subcommittee and moved that it be reported to the full committee. The motion was defeated.
>
> The subcommittee then agreed to hold hearings and Senator Hennings moved that these should begin on February 12 and be limited to two weeks, after which the subcommittee should act on the bills immediately. This motion was defeated.
>
> Hearings by the subcommittee did begin on February 14 and

> ended after three weeks on March 5. On March 19, the subcommittee approved S.83 and reported it, along with majority and minority views, to the full committee.
>
> On April 1, in the full committee, Senator Hennings moved that the Judiciary Committee dispose of civil rights legislation by April 15. He was unable to obtain a vote on this motion.
>
> On April 8, Senator Hennings intended to renew his motion, but there was no meeting of the committee owing to the absence of a quorum.
>
> On April 15, Senator Hennings moved that S.83 be voted on by May 6. The committee took no action.
>
> On May 13, at the next meeting, Senator Hennings desired to move that the committee meet every morning and all day, when the rules of the Senate permitted, and in the evenings if necessary, so that a vote on the bill could be taken by May 16. He was unable to obtain recognition to make this motion.
>
> On June 3 the committee added the sweeping "jury trial" amendment to the bill . . . [an amendment which crippled the voting rights protections by requiring a jury to pass on contempt cases for violations of the bill. Southern juries were not expected to convict for civil rights offenses.]
>
> On June 10 and June 17, Senator Hennings was unable to gain recognition during committee meetings.[2]

It was in 1957, however, that the first major step was taken to overcome the veto power of the Senate Judiciary Committee on civil rights legislation. On June 18, 1957, Eisenhower's civil rights bill, only slightly amended, was passed by a vote of 286 to 126 in the House. When the bill was brought before the Senate, a little-used section of the rule book was employed by a bipartisan, pro-civil rights coalition to achieve their purpose of by-passing the Senate Judiciary Committee. Rule XIV provides that "every bill and joint resolution of the House of Representatives which shall have received a first and second reading without being referred to a committee, shall, if objection be made to further proceeding thereon, be placed on the Calendar . . . [without being sent to committee]." Senator William B. Knowland, Republican minority leader, made objection at the appropriate point. After a debate upon the legitimacy of the procedure, the Senate, in a crucial roll call, defeated a challenging point of order by Richard Russell (D., Georgia) by a vote of 45 to 39. Of particular significance in this action was the voting lineup.[3] The conservative Republican-Southern Democratic coalition, which had been invincible on civil rights issues (particularly procedural ones), was splintered and defeated by a cooperative effort between northern Democrats and liberal Republicans. This vote represented a marked departure from another Senate tradition. The sanctity of committee authority is one of the more revered attitudes of that body, and the deliberate by-passing of the Judiciary Committee was a direct challenge to the authority of Chairman James Eastland. This liberal victory at the committee level was substantially undercut by subsequent action on the floor, but procedurally one barrier had been effectively overcome. Even though the bill emerged substantially without teeth, a civil rights bill was finally brought to the Senate floor.

1960

In 1960 the major civil rights bill in the Senate had to do with voting privileges. This was an election year. Both parties were seeking to present a strong posture in regard to civil rights. The Civil Rights Commission (created by the 1957 Act) had recommended federal voting registrars to end Negro disfranchisement. In the Senate the spate of bills introduced to provide for some form of federal voting registrars got a quick and enthusiastic reception. Because these bills were formally classified as dealing with federal elections, they were referred to the Committee on Rules and Administration, whose chairman was none other than the long-suffering Senator Hennings. The Judiciary Committee was again effectively by-passed. Later in that same session, a diluted omnibus civil rights bill came over from the House. This *was* referred by the leadership to the Senate Judiciary Committee—*but with a proviso that the committee would report the bill back to the Senate floor within five days.* Whether Lyndon Johnson's desire to win the presidential nomination was the key to this maneuver, or whether it was the effect of the increasing power of civil rights groups in northern states, is impossible to measure. But in any case, party leadership overcame a powerful Senate committee.

1964

By 1964 the weakness of the Judiciary Committee's role was patent. Senator Mansfield, the majority leader, invoking the same rule XIV procedure that had been used in 1957, objected to having the House-passed bill referred to the Judiciary Committee, and was sustained by the Chair. The 1964 bill was placed directly on the Senate calendar. On a vote of 54 to 37, the Senate upheld the ruling of the chair when it was challenged by Senator Russell (D., Georgia). Then, having made his point, Mansfield requested unanimous consent to have the bill referred to the Judiciary Committee instructing it to report it back by March 4 *without recommendation or amendment.* The magnanimity of this gesture was not appreciated by Senator Eastland, who refused the offer as an insult to his status as committee chairman.

1965

The 1965 Act, perhaps the most important civil rights legislation since the Civil War, was almost anticlimactic. This was the bill which finally gave teeth to the federal enforcement of voting rights. It required the suspension of literacy and constitutional interpretation tests (which Civil Rights Commission investigations had shown to be widely used in a discriminatory manner) in states where less than 50 percent of the voting-age population was registered or had voted in 1964 (essentially seven southern states), and provided for the appointment of federal enrolling officers to register residents of affected areas.

On March 17, by an overwhelming vote of 67-13, the Senate bill was referred to the Judiciary Committee with instructions to report back by April 9. In the Judiciary Committee the civil rights forces won further victories, broadening and strengthening the coverage of the bill. A group of nine liberals, six Democrats and three Republicans, now held firm numerical control of the committee; and they engineered amendments substantially increasing the power of the federal enrolling officers, providing federal poll watchers, making private citizens as well as public officials liable to the Act's criminal penalties, and banning the poll tax in state and local elections.

Not all of these amendments successfully ran the complete legislative gauntlet. What was significant was that they were able to emerge from the Senate Judiciary Committee, which less than a decade earlier had been the graveyard of civil rights legislation. Civil rights forces no longer had to by-pass the Committee; by 1965 they had tamed it.

The Senate Floor Stage—Breaking the Filibuster

The shifts in power in and surrounding Senate committee deliberations were paralleled on the Senate floor. It is unnecessary to review the long and dramatic history of the Senate filibuster. It is sufficient to note that provision for curbing the right of unlimited debate in the Senate was first made during World War I. In 1917 the Senate adopted rule XXII, which in its present form provides that debate may be ended by a procedure that begins with the filing of a petition signed by sixteen senators. This petition must be brought to a vote on the second day after it has been filed. If the petition is approved by a vote of two-thirds of the senators present and voting, cloture is invoked, and thereafter each senator may speak for only one additional hour on the measure, after which the question before the Senate must be put to a vote. The simple effect of the cloture rule has been that civil rights legislation—in contrast to most other legislation, which is handled through routine, unanimous-consent agreements limiting time for debate—has required not just a majority vote, but the two-thirds vote necessary to overcome an almost inevitable southern filibuster.

Changes in rule XXII to reduce the voting requirement for ending debate is discouraged by the fact that a filibuster can be waged on the issue of whether to change the filibuster rule. Indeed, between 1949 and 1959, section 3 of the rule provided that on a motion to proceed to the consideration of a change in the rules, there could be no limitation on debate at all, not even by two-thirds vote.[4]

Because of these safeguards surrounding rule XXII, the only way in which change can be accomplished is by a motion at the beginning of a Congress that the Senate adopt new rules. For success this motion needs a ruling from the Chair, or a vote of the Senate, on a point of order: that the Senate's rules may be changed at the beginning of the Congress by majority vote. Unfortunately a widely accepted Senate tradition holds that since only one-third of Senate members are elected every two years, the Senate is a continuing body, and Senate rules carry over from one session to the next as a matter of course.

1957

In 1957 when the motion was made at the beginning of the 85th Congress to proceed to the consideration of new rules, the majority leader immediately sought recognition. Since an unwritten rule of the Senate requires recognition of the majority and minority floor leaders before any other senator seeking to speak, the majority leader was able to move to table the motion and bring on a vote without a formal ruling from the Chair. Vice President Nixon had indicated that he would have ruled in the affirmative on the question of whether rules changes could be made by majority vote. Not surprisingly, the tabling motion carried and the attempt at rules change was defeated. But the significance of the skirmish lay in the size of the vote against tabling (and the rules change). Forty-one of the ninety-six senators were opposed to the tabling motion. With a favorable ruling from the Chair and the switch of only seven votes, then, the filibuster rule could have been modified.

As the battle over the 1957 Civil Rights Act was to show, the southern bloc took the warning to heart. Instead of waging an all-out filibuster in an effort to kill the bill, they used the threat of a filibuster to wring concessions from the civil rights forces. Senator Herman Talmadge (D., Georgia) noted on the floor of the Senate, in response to criticism leveled at the southern bloc for their failure to filibuster, that such action might well have provoked a rules change "to impose gag rule at will." Prophetically he continued, "Should we destroy what good will remains among independent Senators . . . the passage of new, radical civil rights legislation . . . will be a foregone conclusion."[5]

On August 7 the roll call on final passage was 72-18. The bill that passed was an emasculated one, but it was the first omnibus civil rights bill to pass both houses in eighty years.

1959

The 86th Congress began with minor changes in rule XXII, but no strong civil rights legislation emerged from the first session in 1959. One interesting event, however, did occur. The Civil Rights Commission was scheduled to go out of existence at the end of the year. All bills for renewal were trapped in committee. Furthermore the Commission had recently issued its 1959 report calling for the appointment of federal officials to register voters in states where the Commission found discrimination, and this had made the southerners unhappy and uncooperative. But the leadership of both parties felt that they could not let the Commission die; it had become too well known and had established too respectable a reputation. Just before the House-passed mutual security (or foreign aid) bill was brought to the floor, the Senate Appropriations Committee approved an amendment to the bill extending the life of the Civil Rights Commission for two years. President pro tem Carl Hayden moved to suspend the rules to permit the legislation to be added to the appropriations bill, and the requisite two-thirds vote was achieved for rules suspension, 71-18. Thereafter the mutual security bill with its unrelated amendment passed the Senate 64-25. The House leadership induced Judge Smith to permit the bill to come to the floor for House concurrence in the amended bill, and the Civil Rights Commission was saved. The whole event was a graphic display of the power of the leadership, when it wished, to achieve rapid action even in the field of civil rights.

1960

When the second session opened, the prospects for some kind of legislation were improved. Nineteen-sixty was an election year. Furthermore, the Civil Rights Commission recommendation for federal voting registrars to end Black disfranchisement had developed widespread interest. Attorney General Rogers had announced that the Administration would be sending Congress an addition to its pending 1959 proposals in the form of a plan for court-appointed voting referees.

In the Senate the spate of bills introduced to provide for some form of federal voting registrars got a quick and enthusiastic reception. As noted above, since they were formally classified as bills dealing with federal elections, they were referred to Senator Hennings' Committee on Rules and Administration.

Toward the end of the previous session, while all civil rights bills were effectively mired in committee, the majority leader had promised on the floor that in the second session on February 15 civil rights would become the pending business of Congress. On that morning there was no indication of how Senator Johnson would keep his pledge. At the end of preliminaries to the start of the day's session, the majority leader routinely asked unanimous consent to proceed to the consideration of a minor measure entitled "A Bill to authorize the Secretary of the Army to lease a portion of Fort Crowder, Mo., to Stella Reorganized School R-1, Mo." There was, of course, no objection. And then the plan was revealed: the majority leader explained that it was this bill which he hoped would be used to begin the discussion of civil rights. "The bill is open to amendment. I hope all interested senators will offer, in a spirit of constructive, responsible, and nonpartisan dedication to human rights, the proposals they believe will best serve the ends of protecting the constitutional rights of American citizens."[6] Thereupon Senator Dirksen took the floor to introduce an amendment embodying the seven-point Administration proposal plus the more recent voter referee plan. Senator Russell was on his feet with an angry complaint against the unusual procedure. "We are the only minority which is not supposed to have any rights whatsoever."[7] One right that the South claimed, of course, was that of the filibuster, and Senator Russell vowed to use it. Senator Johnson, however, was making a bid for the Democratic presidential nomination. A public interpretation of him as a southern politician was one of the chief obstacles he had to overcome. When the filibuster began, Johnson announced that he would use drastic measures to break it. Beginning on February 29, he called the Senate into twenty-four-hour round-the-clock session. If the southerners were to hold the floor to prevent action on the Stella bill as amended, they would have to do so without a break.

But the burden of breaking the well-organized filibuster fell more heavily upon its opponents who had to remain in the Senate building at all times to answer quorum calls to prevent adjournment. The southerners, except for the few actually speaking on the floor, could relax. After nine days the round-the-clock effort was abandoned, and in extended encounters the South wore down the pro-civil rights forces to the point where a series of compromises were ultimately required. Finally, a House-passed bill was sufficiently altered to make it a measure the South could live with, and it passed the Senate on April 8 by a vote of 71-18. While the Senate majority and minority leaders congratulated each other on the passage of civil rights legislation, and Senator Russell claimed victory for the South, other members differed over whether the measure had been one of balanced progress or a sham whose cumbersome procedures would do little to protect Black voting rights in the South.

1963

The years 1961 and 1962 were largely uneventful times for civil rights on Capitol Hill. The biennial attempt at rules change, unaided by the Administration, failed. The Administration did succeed in securing congressional endorsement of a constitutional amendment to ban the poll tax in federal elections, but a bill to modify the literacy test for voting was killed by filibuster.

The year 1963 began, too, with an unsuccessful assault on rule XXII, but this time President Kennedy did send a civil rights package to Congress. Relatively modest, it included some broadening of existing voting rights protections, aid to districts having problems with desegregation, and a four-year extension of the Civil Rights Commission.

But this was a year of racial demonstrations. In April Birmingham began to reach the front pages as Martin Luther King and Fred Shuttlesworth led a drive to achieve equal rights. In May protest marches were broken up by police dogs and fire hoses, and reaction came from all around the world. In April William Moore was shot to death while walking with a sign that said "Equal Rights For All." In June Medgar Evers was murdered in Mississippi, and about the same time the National Guard was ordered to Cambridge, Maryland, to preserve order in racial demonstrations.

On June 11 President Kennedy made a national television address in which he talked of the "fires of frustration [that] are burning in every city, North and South, where legal remedies are not at hand." A week later, after a series of White House meetings with leaders of religious, labor, civil rights, and other organized groups, a much strengthened civil rights proposal was sent to supplement the bills already before Congress. Besides strengthening already existing protections and reviving powerful sections deleted from previous bills, the Administration measure included sweeping new provisions to prohibit discrimination in public accommodations (hotels, restaurants, etc.) and to permit administrators to cut off federal grants-in-aid for any state programs administered discriminatorily. Although not a part of the Administration bill, an FEPC provision creating an Equal Employment Opportunity Commission was also endorsed by the President.

In the Senate, Majority Leader Mansfield introduced a measure including the full administration package, and he and Dirksen cosponsored one which included everything but the public accommodations section, a section which the Minority Leader did not, at that time, approve.[8] Senator Warren Magnuson (D., Washington), introduced a separate public accommodations bill, whose constitutional basis was explicitly stated to be the Commerce Clause. While the other measures were referred to Senator Eastland's uncooperative committee, the Magnuson measure went to his own Interstate and Foreign Commerce Committee for more sympathetic treatment.

But the strategy of the Administration was to wait for House passage of an omnibus bill, and major attention therefore was focused on the question of what Congressman Celler's subcommittee and full

Judiciary Committee would report out. To this part of the story we shall return. It is sufficient here to recall that on November 22, Lee Harvey Oswald fired a rifle in Dallas, and the President was dead. Speaking to a joint session of Congress and a shocked and grieving world five days later, President Johnson said: "No memorial oration or eulogy could more eloquently honor President Kennedy's memory than the earliest possible passage of the civil rights bill for which he fought so long."

1964

A few weeks later, in early 1964, a strong bill passed the House. The dangers in the Senate, however, were severe. Southern senators, led by their strategist Richard Russell of Georgia, had vowed a fight to the finish. And Senate Minority Leader Everett McKinley Dirksen, who would have to deliver close to two dozen Republican votes if cloture was to be voted, warned that the House measure was too broad to attract many of those needed minority votes.

As we have seen, Senator Mansfiield, under rule XIV procedure, placed the bill directly on the Senate calendar. Taking a bill from the calendar to bring it before the Senate for consideration is ordinarily done during the Morning Hour by a motion which is not subject to debate. Senator Russell, however, blocked that procedure by insisting on the reading of the Journal of the previous day's action, and then talked for an hour on an amendment to the Journal. By that time it was past 2 P.M., the time at which the Senate rules require the Morning Hour to end. Thereafter, the motion to take up a bill becomes debatable, and for the next three weeks debate on the civil rights bill was formally a debate on whether the bill should be debated at all. On March 26 the southerners relented, and allowed a vote to be taken. By 67-17, the civil rights bill became the pending business of the Senate.

Effective organization was apparent on both sides of the filibuster effort. Senator Russell had divided his eighteen colleagues into three teams, two of which could be absent at any given time while the third was responsible for holding the floor. Such systematic exploitation of the virtually unlimited debate allowed by the Senate rules was nothing new to the Senate. What was novel was the high degree of counter organization established by bipartisan supporters of the bill. Under the captaincy of the assistant floor leaders of both parties (Democratic Senator Hubert H. Humphrey of Minnesota and Republican Senator Thomas H. Kuchel of California) a system of assignments was set up to insure a quorum and to allocate defense of the many sections of the 55-page measure. Coordination to offset absences because of out-of-town engagements was achieved; twice-daily strategy sessions for the Senators, staff, and Justice Department officials were held; and a daily newsletter informing the participating senators of the day's activities was published.

The strategy of the southerners was one of total delay and obstruction, a gamble for total victory or the nearest thing to it. Unlike the Acts of '57 and '60, this was not a bill they felt they could accept. And tactically the South believed the coalition of sixty-seven senators needed to invoke cloture a highly unlikely one. The longer a vote could be postponed, the better they thought the chance would be that the enthusiastic liberals and the somewhat unwilling conservatives would begin to quarrel.

In retrospect it would appear that an attempt by the southerners to trade early passage for some of the bill's "teeth" would have achieved a more satisfactory result for them. For starting about the fifth week of debate, negotiation among Senator Dirksen, Administration senators, and officials of the Justice Department and White House began to bring results in the form of a revised bill that would effectively win the support of the Republican votes needed for cloture. Although Dirksen's amendments were seventy in number, few of them went to the substance of the bill. The most important changes were made in the public accommodations and fair employment sections of the bill. Their import was to require a "pattern of discriminatory practice" before the attorney general could intervene, rather than simply a single instance, and to permit a grace period for state and local attempts to combat discrimination before the federal mechanism could go into effect in states which had similar laws of their own. These changes caused some liberal dissatisfaction, but they did not come close to satisfying the southerners.

The form of the revised proposal was hammered out between May 11 and 16, and on May 19 the bill was presented at party caucuses. Then on May 26 Senator Dirksen introduced the substitute bill and put his full weight behind it. "We have now reached the point where there must be action; and I trust that there will be action. I believe this is a salable piece of work. . . . "[9] Just a few weeks earlier Senator Dirksen had made clear that he felt the bill was too strong, that he would not back a measure which included a compulsory employment discrimination ban or whose public accommodations section was so broad. But now he obviously had come around to the other side, for the amendments he had achieved in the bill did not meet his original objections.

The conversion of Senator Dirksen, ordinarily considered a conservative, to the cause of civil rights typifies the changing consensus on this issue perhaps as much as anything else in these events. As Dirksen explained at a press conference on May 19, "No army is stronger than an idea whose time has come. . . . Let editors rave at will and let states fulminate at will, but the time has come, and it can't be stopped."[10]

With a few final compromises out of the way, the historic cloture vote was taken on June 10. Eleven weeks had passed since the measure was first placed before the Senate and the preliminary filibuster had begun, and eight weeks had elapsed since the southerners had permitted the bill to become the pending business of the Senate. During the second period virtually no other business had been transacted. The debate throughout had been germane to the bill, and most of the time the atmosphere in the Senate chamber had been calm and amicable.

In the final hour before the vote, Senators Mansfield, Russell, Humphrey, and Dirksen summarized their positions. At 2 P.M. came the vote that ended the unbroken tradition of the Senate that cloture could never be achieved in the United States Senate on a civil rights issue. Seventy-one senators voted for the motion, eleven after having been on the other side in past years, seven of them quite adamantly so. Among the twenty-nine votes in opposition were five Republicans and two Democrats from small population midwest and western states and three Democrats from border states, as well as the nineteen senators who had waged the filibuster.

Thereafter, mopping-up operations took the next few days, as over one hundred amendments pending at the time of cloture were called up to be defeated—in most instances by overwhelming margins. On June 19, the final vote was taken, and the Senate passed the 1964 Civil Rights Bill by a 73-27 margin, one year after President Kennedy had sent it to the Hill. More important than passage itself, perhaps, was the fact that the ultimate Senate barrier to civil rights legislation, the filibuster, had been surmounted.

1965

On the powerful Voting Rights Bill of 1965, floor action in the Senate began officially on April 13. There was no southern filibuster or debate on the motion to take up the bill. Mansfield had threatened to hold the Senate in session over the Easter recess if such tactics were tried, and the southerners cooperated. After a poll tax ban had been defeated, the way was rapidly cleared for passage. When the southern bloc refused to agree to a limitation of debate by unanimous consent, Senator Mansfield announced that a cloture petition would be filed in two days, and on May 25 the Senate voted cloture by a margin of 70-30 after only four weeks of debate. The next day the bill was passed 77-19.

There was no sense of history being made in the Senate chamber as there had been the previous year when cloture was voted. What had been the shattering of an unbroken tradition the year before had become virtually routine.

Civil Rights in the House of Representatives

The story of civil rights legislation in the House of Representatives over the decade from the mid-1950's to the mid-1960's can be told with far greater dispatch. In the late 1950's token civil rights legislation had little difficulty emerging from the lower chamber. This was partly because the House Judiciary subcommittee, which reviewed civil rights legislation, was under the chairmanship of a northern liberal, Congressman Emanuel Celler of Brooklyn, also chairman of the full Judiciary Committee; partly because a bipartisan coalition of middle-road Democrats and Eisenhower Republicans formed the full committee's substantive majority; and partly because a similar coalition dominated the floor. Generally favorable action on Eisenhower's civil rights recommendations emerged in 1956, 1957, and 1959, at both the committee and floor stages. Both more conservative and more liberal forces were successfully beaten back at every stage of consideration. Even the Rules Committee, chaired by Representative Howard W. Smith of Virginia, a southern conservative, after a series of complex parliamentary maneuvers and inordinate delays, permitted fairly unrestricted floor action. This was in part because the presidential proposals as modified by the full Judiciary Committee were tame, in part because of a sullen faith on the part of the conservative coalition on the Rules Committee that no strong civil rights bill could possibly emerge from the Senate even if passed by the House.

1959-1960

The first dramatic struggle came in the 86th Congress. Action in the House began with hearings before the House Judiciary Subcommittee Number Five, and on June 17, 1959, the subcommittee approved a strengthened version of a measure supported by the Administration. In the full Judiciary Committee, the bill was substantially trimmed back, with several of the key provisions of the Administration measure eliminated. Along with dissenting reports by southerners (who considered the measure an unconstitutional infringement of states' rights) and liberals (who felt it was ineffective), the measure was reported out and was sent to the Rules Committee on August 20. There it languished until the first session closed, despite efforts of Emanuel Celler to bring pressure for a resolution clearing it for floor action. Celler, while not enthusiastic about the bill in its then present form, felt that once on the floor it could be used as a vehicle for strengthening amendments.

Toward the end of the session, other efforts having proved unsuccessful, Congressman Celler attempted to dislodge the bill from Rules Committee jurisdiction by filing a discharge petition. The discharge petition is a device which, if signed by a majority of the members of the House, brings a bill out of a committee and to the floor for debate and action. Although the procedure seems simple enough, the decision to put one's signature on the petition is not lightly made. Incurring the displeasure of the Rules Committee can result in the interment or delay of a member's future legislative proposals. In consequence, by the second session of the 86th Congress, although the petition to discharge the Civil Rights Bill had attracted a sizable number of signatures, it was still far from the needed 219 names.

At this point the Democratic Study Group (a group of like-minded liberals) decided to take unprecedented action. Believing that constituent pressure would force nonsigners to sign if only their failure to do so were made known, the DSG assigned each of its members the task of checking a number of names on the petition. (The petition was accessible to members at the Speaker's desk). When the members of the DSG had assembled a complete list of the 175 signers, they released it to the *New York Times.* The *Times* reported the devastating statistic that only 30 of the 175 names were those of Republicans. In an election year this was dynamite. The timing of this release coincided with a statement from Speaker Rayburn approving the discharge petition as the way to get action on the bill. The number of signatories climbed and the Rules Committee capitulated when the list was less than ten names from achieving a majority.

Once a bill has been cleared for floor action by the Rules Committee, it is often debated and amended by the House sitting as a Committee of the Whole, a procedure favored because of its flexible rules and the absence of roll-call voting. For this bill the Committee of the Whole was chaired by Congressman Francis Walter of Pennsylvania, whose loyalty to the leadership was demonstrated by the strictness of his rulings on what amendments were germane to the bill. Walter successfully stymied liberal efforts to strengthen the bill and southern efforts to cripple it, and thereafter, on March 24, 1960, by a vote of 211-109, the House passed and sent to the Senate the Civil Rights Bill of 1960.

1963-1964

As noted above, the first major civil rights program of the Kennedy Administration was introduced in January 1963 at the beginning of the 88th Congress. In the House the program was initially referred to Congressman Celler's Subcommittee Five of the Judiciary Committee. In August the subcommittee completed its hearings and marked up the Administration measure to achieve a substantial strengthening of the Kennedy proposals. Once again, however, full committee action brought a weakening of the subcommittee product, but the measure finally sent to the Rules Committee in November was still a stronger measure than the Administration request. On December 5, after President Kennedy's assassination and Lyndon Johnson's call for a strong civil rights bill as an appropriate memorial to the martyred President, Chairman Howard Smith of the Rules Committee announced that he would schedule hearings on granting clearance to the bill.

In January 1964, during the ten hours of floor debate on the bill, the House experienced some of the most intense lobbying efforts of modern legislative history.[11] Pressure tactics were coordinated by the Leadership Conference on Civil Rights, an association of seventy-nine civil rights, labor, church, and other assorted organizations. For the House debate, literally thousands of Conference members came to Washington to mount a massive effort to insure defeat of expected southern amendments to the bill. Individual members seated in the galleries were assigned congressmen to watch. If at any time during the debate a spotter noticed one of his assigned congressmen absent for any length of time, he went to a telephone and called a temporary Leadership Conference headquarters established in the nearby Congressional Hotel. From there a call went out to two Leadership Conference volunteers at a telephone in a friendly congressman's office nearest to the office of the absentee. Within moments the delinquent representative would be visited with a request to return to the floor to be on hand for votes which could come at any time.

Another aspect of this successful legislative campaign was its close tie-in with the Democratic Study Group. The DSG at first supplemented and then replaced the Leadership Conference's spotter system with a "buddy" system of its own. Legislative strategy was developed by the floor manager of the bill, Representative Celler, and by a special DSG civil rights steering committee, headed by Representative Richard Bolling (D., Missouri). Every morning before the session began, skull sessions were held in Representative Frank Thompson's office (D., New Jersey). These were usually attended by two or three key staff of the Leadership Conference, Lawrence O'Brien or someone else from his White House liaison staff, and members of the DSG. During floor debate on the measure, Attorney General Katzenbach, Burke Marshall of the Civil Rights Division, and several other Justice Department attorneys were present in the galleries at all times. Whenever problems arose as amendments came up, Bolling or an associate would signal to the galleries and Katzenbach, Leadership Conference lobbyists, and the representatives would huddle just off the floor of the House to determine their course of action.

Republican efforts for the bill were coordinated chiefly by Republican members of the Judiciary Committee, particularly Congressmen McCulloch of Ohio and Lindsay of New York, aided by the minority Judiciary counsel and the staff of the Republican Legislative Research Association.

On the opposite side of the issue, forces were comparatively unorganized and, in comparison with southern bloc efforts in the past, almost dispirited. The southern whip system appeared to be inoperative throughout most of the debate. Chief strategist Edwin Willis (D., Louisiana) was without staff aid on the floor. Strategy sessions were informal and infrequent compared with the continuous efforts of the civil rights forces. The Coordinating Committee for Fundamental American Freedoms, whose chairman was William Loeb, publisher of the right-wing Manchester, New Hampshire, *Union Leader*, was formed for the specific purpose of defeating the act, but its efforts were largely confined to attempts at influencing public opinion. Its financial support came almost entirely from the Mississippi Sovereignty Commission, and it was unable to enlist participation by business interests which formerly could have been expected to oppose government interference of the kind implicit in the public accommodations and equal opportunity sections of the bill.

The result of these efforts was overwhelming passage of the bill—unscathed by the 122 amendments which were offered to it. Although 28 amendments were accepted, most were technical improvements. Not a single one of those adopted was opposed by the bill's managers. The vote on final passage, taken on February 10, 1964, was 290-130, and the bill was sent to the Senate. Northern Democrats had supported it 141 to 4; Republicans supported it 138 to 34; and even the Southern Democrats contributed 11 votes (out of their possible 103) to the winning side.

On June 22, 1964, after the historic defeat of the southern filibuster, the Civil Rights Bill, as amended by the Senate, was returned to the Speaker's desk in the House. Representative Celler moved that it be directly taken up and approved by the House. Such a procedure required unanimous consent because it short-circuited the usual requirement of a rule granted by the Rules Committee. Unanimous consent was blocked.

Under Rules Committee procedures the chairman is required to schedule a meeting within seven days of his receipt of a signed request by three members of the committee; otherwise a majority may themselves call a meeting. Representatives Madden (D., Indiana), Sisk (D., California), and Young (D., Texas) used the former procedure to force the chairman to call a meeting for June 30. At that meeting, a rare humiliation was administered to one of the most powerful chairmen in the House, "Judge" Smith.

Smith sought delay by holding lengthy hearings. When Representative Madden moved to get a committee vote at 5 P.M., the Chairman ruled the motion out of order because the committee was not in executive session. Thereupon the committee voted 6-4 to go into executive session, and approved the 5 P.M. termination of discussion 7-4. Then the majority of the committee voted to limit debate on the bill in the House to one hour. As a final assurance against delay, they voted 8-5 to take the presentation of the committee resolution out of the hands of the Chairman and authorized Madden to handle it.

On July 2 the House voted to accept the bill as amended by the Senate 289-126, with virtually the same lineup as in the 290-130 vote for House passage on February 10. Only six members switched sides from one vote to the other, three in each direction. One of those who changed his vote from opposition to support was Representative Charles L. Weltner, Democrat of Atlanta, Georgia. In a speech explaining his vote, he told the House that he would vote "to accept the verdict of the nation . . . " "I will add my voice to those who seek reasoned and conciliatory adjustment to a new reality, and . . . I would urge that we at home now move on to the unfinished task of building a new South. We must not remain forever bound to another lost cause."[12]

1965

In 1965 subcommittee and full committee action in the House, as in the Senate, resulted in strengthening amendments to the already powerful administration voting rights bill introduced by Representative Emanuel Celler. Speaker McCormack gave his public approval to the House committee action.

When the bill was sent to the Rules Committee in early June, the liberals effectively exercised their continued command of both parliamentary tactics and voting majority to force clearance for floor action just four weeks after the bill had been reported from Judiciary.

On July 6, 7, and 8, floor debate took place, and the only real contest was between the Celler bill and a Republican substitute only slightly less potent. The shakiness of the once solid South was much in evidence when less than half the southern representatives followed the tactical suggestion of their leaders that they vote for the Republican substitute. (In 1960 Representative Smith had been able to lead a virtually unanimous southern block through a series of intricate votes which came very near to scuttling the key provisions of the 1960 act.)

The vote on final passage revealed even more. The Celler bill had emerged entirely unscathed from debate in the Committee of the Whole, including even the poll tax ban (which was subsequently to be softened in conference). Yet the vote on July 9 found 3 southern Republicans and 35 Southern Democrats, mostly from urban areas with sizable Negro populations, joining 302 Northerners to pass the bill 388-85.

Perhaps the words of Georgia's Representative Weltner the previous year had been heeded. Or perhaps it was the lesson of the 1964 elections being learned; for all of the 12 Southern Democrats who had voted for the 1964 Civil Rights Bill had been re-elected, and 14 out of the 34 Republicans who had voted against it had been defeated. Certainly the prospect of increased Black registration and the new national consensus favoring strong civil rights legislation must also have played a part. But whatever the complex of reasons, the Judiciary Committee, the Rules Committee, and the floor of the House had, by 1965, become significantly more friendly to effective civil rights proposals than was the case even a few years earlier.

In both houses, centripetal forces had demonstrated their capacity to overcome the traditional power of an inverted coalition led by strategically placed committee chairmen.

CONGRESS AND CIVIL RIGHTS: 1965-1968

The story of civil rights legislation after 1965 in both Houses is mixed. In 1966 and 1967, virtually no civil rights legislation emerged. In the election year of 1968, and under enormous pressure from President Johnson, a comprehensive civil rights bill was passed as a capstone to the arch of civil rights protections constructed in the Congress between 1956 and 1965. The omnibus 1968 act strengthened laws prohibiting violent interference with the exercise by minorities of specified civil rights including voting, attending a public school or college, obtaining services at public accommodations, serving on state or federal juries, obtaining employment, using a public facility, participating in federally assisted programs, or riding on a public carrier; prohibited discrimination in the sale or rental of all housing in the United States in three progressive stages; outlawed discrimination in the financing of housing; prohibited discriminatory practices by real estate brokers; barred "block-busting"; and authorized the Attorney General to bring suits against patterns or practices of housing discrimination.*

Substantively the 1968 act was impressive in scope and in enforcement provisions. Strategically, in terms of internal manifestations of congressional power, the act was anticlimactical. The major procedural barriers to this kind of legislation had been stripped away in the decade 1956-1965.

But looking at congressional inaction on civil rights issues in 1966 and 1967, and at recent cutbacks in congressional appropriations for executive enforcement of civil rights provisions already on the books in such fields as education and employment practices, it is clear that counterpressures are being felt by congressional leadership (and followership) in both parties.

One fact, however, emerges from the past fifteen years with stunning clarity: the future of federal civil rights policy will no longer be determined by a southern minority in the Congress. The moral and political burden of solving our greatest national problem has been shifted to the back of the nation's majority.

---

*Some of the language in this paragraph is borrowed directly from the *Congressional Quarterly Weekly Report,* No. 16, Vol. XXVI, April 19, 1968, pp. 851-2.

Chapter VII

HOUND DOG AND WATCH DOG: THE EXERCISE OF PLURALISTIC POWER

If centripetal forces of President and party have become increasingly powerful elements in the dynamics of general law-making, centrifugal and semi-autonomous forces still dominate much of the remaining business of the congressional system. This is especially true in the investigating (hound dog) and surveillance (watch dog) functions of Congress—in the attempts of congressmen to illuminate social evils by inquiry and to control or influence bureaucratic practice by a variety of devices. Even more than its power to legislate, congressional powers to appropriate, to investigate, to mediate, to alleviate, and to repudiate give Congress its special role in the American governmental system.

There is a widespread misunderstanding of the hound dog and watch dog functions of Congress. A generation of political-science writing comes to the virtually unanimous conclusion that Congress often performs these badly and irresponsibly.[1] The argument is that:

—on many matters, the bureaucratic agenda is too long, involved, and complex to permit effective congressional oversight (e.g., the length of the foreign service and military promotions lists; the complexity of international finance policy; the technical character of space budgets);

—Strategically situated congressmen use their right to investigate social evils and their power to influence bureaucratic decisions only to feather parochial or personal nests (e.g, Chairman Rivers [D., South Carolina] of the House Armed Services Committee using his power to insure a heavy federal investment in defense industries in the Charleston area; the late Senator Joseph McCarthy [R., Wisconsin] using his investigatory powers to feed his own insatiable ego);

—even when disinterested, the views of a chairman of a committee or subcommittee are more likely to reflect untutored and simplistic biases than are the views of a department secretary or a President.

These conclusions of political scientists, however valid within a limited context, miss the basic point. It is the *general* power of Congress to act as watch dog and hound dog, not particular exercises of that power, which constitute the basic value of our legislature to our national life and to freedom. And as Professor Schattschneider once said, "If you examine a mountain with a microscope, the mountain disappears." Whatever inadequacies, deficiencies, and abuses show up in any specific illustration of congressional investigations and oversight (and there are many), the overwhelming reality is that our government bureaucracy and our society generally behave more honestly, more circumspectly, and more humanely because of these congressional powers. A simple review of governments and societies abroad which have no such protections is sufficient proof of this postulate. The major force of congressional influence is in what Carl Friedrich once called "the law of anticipated reaction." In other words, if the bureaucracy or the society misbehaves, Congress *can* call it to account. The reality and the threat of legislative surveillance and investigation derive from congressional powers to advise and consent, to make laws, to appropriate monies, and finally and ultimately, to impeach high executive and judicial officers. Those who say that the impeachment power is not important because it has been used so infrequently again miss a point. Constitutional authority is a vast source of latent—and hence real—power.

Formal Investigations

The hound dog and watch dog functions of Congress constitute a continuous process conducted by a wide variety of means: standing committee hearings, special requests to the executive branch for information, staff studies, annual and special reports, audits by the General

Accounting Office, appropriations hearings, congressional vetoes over reorganization plans submitted by the President, telephone calls, bean soup luncheons, friendly words of warning, etc. Formal investigations constitute only the more elaborate congressional mechanisms for performing watch dog and hound dog functions; but they are virtually the only means available to Congress for examining social and economic questions from outside the framework of the federal bureaucracy. Taking a leaf from the notebook of British Parliamentary studies of prison reform (1722), chimney sweeps (1817), pauper lunatics (1827), police (1828), and the factory system (1832),[2] the U. S. Congress has over the past century investigated a wide variety of social and economic problems of national consequence. These have included studies of Black migration from South to North (1880), immigration of foreign contract labor (1888), strikebreaking by railroads (1892), western land reclamation (1909), banking and finance (1912), communist activities (1930), stock exchange (1931), munitions industry (1934), migratory labor (1937), and monopoly (1939).

Since World War II, Congress has looked at such questions as organized crime, the price of drugs and other commodities, labor racketeering, and more recently, college unrest, nutrition, and aging. Many of these investigations have been of historic importance. They awakened the public conscience; they stimulated Congress to devise or tighten laws. In every case, the hearings are rich sources of historical data about important social and economic problems in this nation's past.

Most formal investigations by Congress, however, have been addressed to the performance of executive departments, agencies, and personnel. The first investigation in 1792 was almost a prototype: an examination of the expedition against Indians in the Ohio Region under Major General Arthur St. Clair. The expedition had ended in disaster. From then until the voluminous investigation into the causes of Pearl Harbor (1945-46), and the more recent investigations of the *Pueblo* incident and thefts of military fuel in Thailand, the conduct of wars has been a favorite subject of congressional investigation. Actually, possibly the worst investigating committee in the nation's history (the Joint Committee on the conduct of the [Civil] War) and the best (the Senate Committee to investigate the National Defense Program in World War II) were both concerned with the effectiveness of the government in waging war.

Formal investigations of federal activities during peacetime have been stimulated usually by some disclosure of incompetence, corruption, or alleged disloyalty. Over the past two decades, for example, investigations have dealt with such issues as federal officials speculating in grains; communists in government agencies; mismanagement in the Atomic Energy Commission; the lending policies of the Reconstruction

Finance Corporation; fraud and irregularities in the Internal Revenue Service; "windfall profits" under F.H.A. mortgage practices; favoritism in the Dixon-Yates power contract; questionable information practices of government agencies; inefficiencies in the Civil Aeronautics Administration; the U. S. lag in missile development; improper conduct in the Federal Communications Commission; waste in government stockpiling; security processes in the Department of State; and the use of lie detectors by federal agents.

Of all fields of investigation, those that have aroused most controversy have been concerned with "loyalty" and "security." Beginning in the 1930's, but reaching their peak in the early 1950's, investigations into un-American activities, disloyalty, and "security risks" have been conducted by a number of select, special, or standing committees of Congress. Although federal personnel have been a central target, many of the investigations in this general area have reviewed "un-American" activities in Hollywood, in radio and television, in labor unions, in foundations, in colleges, in the Ku Klux Klan, etc. The most notorious investigations are associated with the names of Representative Martin Dies (D., Texas), who for years was chairman of the House Un-American Activities Committee; and Senator Joseph McCarthy (R., Wisconsin), who as chairman of the Senate Government Operations Permanent Investigating Subcommittee terrorized individuals, agencies, and a whole nation with wild but unnerving accusations of communism in high places during the early 1950's.

The abuse of individual and committee power in the Congress is nowhere better reflected than in the proceedings of the "Dies Committee" and the "McCarthy Subcommittee." The nature of the abuse is suggested in words used by a scholar to describe the Joint Committee on the Conduct of the War during Lincoln's administration:

> . . . its undocumented insinuations, loud publicity against the reputations of men who are not permitted to defend themselves, its suppression of testimony which did not support the official thesis . . . , its star chamber atmosphere, and its general disregard of the rules of fair procedure. . . . [3]

Out of these latter-day abuses came cries for reform. On March 23, 1955, the House voted on a resolution to establish a minimum standard of conduct for the House committees. At about the same time, a subcommittee of the Senate Rules Committee issued a unanimous report "recommending twelve rules to protect witnesses and to ensure greater majority control in investigations."[4]

These internal reforms and recommendations were abetted by a decision of the U. S. Supreme Court in the Watkins Case.[5] In essence, the Court held that although the "power of the Congress to conduct investigations is inherent in the legislative process," this power is not unlimited, and that "abuses of the investigative process may imperceptibly lead to abridgement of protected freedoms."

It is patent that congressional investigations are conducted not by the Congress as a whole, but by committees, subcommittees, individual chairmen and interested members, and congressional staff. Investigations, therefore, are instruments of segmented power in the Congress. Whatever their social utility, they are frequently newsworthy and are therefore a major instrument for building the status and reputation, and enhancing the powers, of individual congressmen. There is little question, for example, that the skill and fairness with which Senator Harry S. Truman investigated defense production during World War II led to his choice as Vice President on the Democratic ticket in 1944.[6]

What is true of formal investigations tends to be true to a greater or lesser extent of all oversight and surveillance activities of the Congress: the manifestation of pluralistic rather than centralized power in the Congress. To these watch-dog functions we now turn.

Oversight by Spending Controls

No power of Congress is more jealously guarded or more fraught with administrative implications than its constitutional power to control expenditures. Whether Congress in fact wields this power with fairness, skill, and a sense of the public interest is a matter of almost continuous debate within Congress itself, between Congress and the executive, and among academic political scientists. The debate is complicated by a substantial difference of opinion about the appropriate role of Congress in expenditure control, as in other areas of oversight and surveillance. As Keefe and Ogul have suggested, there are two conflicting normative models.[7] The first is that "legislative bodies should set only broad policy and not interfere with the details of administration." The second is that "a primary task of legislative bodies is to further bureaucratic responsibility. The legislative body must be concerned with all policy, both broad and detailed."

If the first model is assumed, Congress performs its expenditure control functions poorly. If the second is assumed, Congress performs only intermittently well. But again it should be emphasized that the very existence of the *power* to authorize and appropriate, even if exercised poorly according to some abstract measure, has a conditioning effect upon executive branch policies and procedures. No administrator knows when he will be called upon to justify a policy or procedure of his agency before a legislative or appropriations committee or subcommittee of the Congress. If this uncertainty promotes a vast amount of record keeping and an occasional timidity in bureaucratic behavior, it also keeps executive agencies on their toes and reminds them that they are ultimately accountable to the people through the Congress as well as through the President. With the assistance of the largest unit in Congress' own bureaucracy, the General Accounting Office, those legislators responsible for authorizations and appropriations are in a position to use their control over expenditures as a powerful instrument of executive branch surveillance, at least in theory.

Alas, congressional practice is not generally commensurate with its theoretical power. Attacks on uses and abuses of the spending power by Congress are legion. Among the most frequent criticisms are these:

—subcommittees put asunder what the Bureau of the Budget has joined together; in consequence, the federal budget, once it leaves the President's office, is never reviewed as a coordinated whole by the Congress or by any subdivision thereof;

—chairmen of powerful committees and subcommittees use their prerogatives to increase or decrease authorizations or appropriations according to whim, with the whim too often determined by parochial prejudices and special interests;

—appropriations subcommittees exercise nonstatutory controls over executive agencies through the language of subcommittee reports, thereby assuming an executive branch prerogative or undercutting general powers of Congress-as-a-whole;

—the insistence of many legislative committees upon annual renewals of authorizations leads to at least four sets of hearings on money bills, two in the Senate and two in the House, with their consequent burden for busy executive officials. (The practice of annual authorizations is defended on the grounds that without them the legislative committees could not perform the surveillance functions mandated by the Legislative Reorganization Act of 1946, and that all effective control over the bureaucracy would be transferred to the appropriations subcommittees.)

—the size of the budget is so vast that subdivisions of Congress, and Congress-as-a-whole, have no means of imposing general wisdom upon its major segments, like Defense. As a result, hearings degenerate into matters of inconsequential detail, such as the relative prices paid by the Marine Corps and the Army for overcoats;

—the enormous decentralization of decision-making on money bills gives "pork barrel" advantages to a select few in the Congress who can imply or suggest that an agency's overall budget will suffer unless a federal installation or contract is pressed in their district;

—the findings of the General Accounting Office are not effectively reviewed by the relevant committees in the expenditures process, so that opportunities are lost to impose financial discipline on waste and inefficiency;

—delays on money bills beyond the beginning of each fiscal year raise havoc with agency planning and administration.

During the 89th Congress, the Joint Committee on the Organization of the Congress took voluminous testimony on the handling of money bills.[8] The Committee made a number of significant recommendations aimed at improving the exercise of the spending power. The committee report and subsequent legislation that passed the Senate (but was blocked in the House) in 1967 called for substantially increased responsibilities to the Comptroller General for aiding Congress in examining expenditure issues; for four-year estimates of executive branch expenditures; and for the more efficient scheduling, and forward planning, of congressional appropriations.

What is clear is that (1) no power of Congress over the executive branch is more fundamental than its control over spending; (2) this control is presently exercised pluralistically, parochially, and episodically; (3) the wise use of the spending power for purposes of administrative oversight is sufficiently important to the proper functioning of the federal government to warrant continuing concern within and outside Congress.

Oversight by Personnel Controls

The two fundamental instruments of control in any organization are budget and personnel. The Congress has the same kind of unsystematic and intermittent control over federal personnel that it has over federal budgets. But again, the *fact* of power in this area is of greater importance than the particular *exercise* of power. At the risk of tediousness, this point must be made again and again. Any fair analysis of the exercise of congressional powers over executive branch personnel would show that these powers have been applied unevenly, sometimes unwisely, and sometimes (as in the case of Senator Joseph McCarthy's witch hunts in the Department of State) disastrously. But the latent as well as real influence of key congressmen over executive branch personnel is a constant reminder to the President and to the department heads that they live in a constitutional system of limited powers internally checked. Perhaps it is only an act of political faith to contend that the freedom of the nation is more safely preserved by the daily exercise of countervailing power (even when occasionally misapplied) than it is by the undiluted exercise of presidential or bureaucratic power checked every quadrennium by the very general mandates of a general election. However rational specific bureaucratic decisions may be, however parochial, misguided, or even selfish the particular actions of powerful congressmen may be, our constitutional faith is that lay politicians can on occasion reflect a higher rationality than bureaucratic experts, and that in any case neither of the two relevant branches of our government has a monopoly on virtue or disinterestedness.

Congressional control over executive branch personnel takes three major forms: Senate confirmation, laws governing the classified services (civil, military and foreign), and informal pressures. These, of course, are in addition to the ultimate weapon of impeachment, a weapon used only twice in American history against officers in the executive branch.

Senate Confirmation

Executive officials subject under the constitution to Senate confirmation include members of the executive branch at the cabinet and assistant secretary level, federal judges, foreign service appointees, members of federal regulatory commissions, military officers, postmasters, and certain other noncareer federal employees.

The extent to which the confirmation power is latent rather than applied is revealed in the fact that out of more than 700,000 nominations made by Presidents Truman, Eisenhower, and Kennedy, only 12 were rejected outright by the Senate, and only 1700 were withdrawn by the President after an appraisal of possible congressional flak. Under Johnson and under Nixon, none has been rejected by formal vote of the Senate, although both Presidents withdrew a number of nominations when it became clear that adamant congressional opposition existed. Ninety percent of all nominations and confirmations concern the military whose jobs are relatively noncontroversial. Even within the remaining 10 percent, the incidence of Senate disapproval is remarkably small. This is owed in part, of course, to presidential pains to clear nominations with key senators in advance of formal submission for confirmation. "Key senators" means not only the chairman and leading members of committees holding confirmation hearings, but also senators from the President's party from whose state the appointee comes. If the President does not consult in advance with the latter, he has violated "senatorial courtesy"—and faces the likelihood that a senator so by-passed will state on the floor that the President's nomination is "personally obnoxious" to him. The protesting senator may expect almost unanimous support against the President from his fellow senators. Today, a backfire on an issue of "senatorial courtesy" can only be considered an example of executive ineptitude—it is, however, true that "senatorial courtesy" narrows somewhat the field of eligibles for executive branch appointment.

It is instructive to note the reasons that certain nominations become controversial: the protections as well as abuses of congressional power are thereby illuminated.

(1) *Conflict of interest*—charges that a man's background and financial holdings so identify him with a particular set of private interests as to make him unfit to occupy an official position charged with regulating or negotiating with those selfsame interests;

(2) *Lack of qualifications*—charges that the nomination was politi-

cally inspired or that the nominee lacked experience in the field to which he had been appointed;

(3) *Disagreement over policy*—charges involving a difference in policy orientation from that held by powerful senators and/or external group interests;

(4) *Communist sympathies*—charges raised mostly during the McCarthy period and often directed at some of America's ablest and most patriotic citizens;

(5) *Personal vendetta*—charges involving political or personality conflicts.

In questioning appointments recommended by President Nixon, individual senators have tended to concentrate on possible conflicts of interest, lack of qualifications, and dubious policy orientations. For example, Secretary of the Interior, Walter J. Hickel, was accused of having had "close connections with the oil industry"; the nomination of Willie Mae Rogers as Assistant to the President for Consumer Affairs was withdrawn after legislative accusations that she was unqualified, since her "consumer protection" activities for *Good Housekeeping* magazine had been a "phoney commercial enterprise"; the appointment of Dr. John Knowles, President Nixon's initial choice to become Assistant Secretary of HEW for Health and Scientific Affairs, was blocked by Senator Dirksen after the American Medical Association had protested Dr. Knowles' views on "public medicine."

It is patent that if nominees are questioned or rejected on conflict-of-interest grounds or because of lack of qualifications, the public interest is being served. If nominees are questioned or rejected because of personal vendettas or wild charges of "communist sympathies," the public interest is not likely to be served. The third category above is the troublesome one. It is here that the continuing struggle between the President and powerful segments of Congress for control of executive branch policy is most in evidence, where ideologies and interests compete and clash most dramatically. An evaluation of saints and sinners depends upon one's perspective. For according to Miles' Law (named for its coiner, Rufus Miles, former administrative assistant secretary of H.E.W.), "Where one stands depends upon where one sits."

Laws Governing the Classified Services

The performance of executive branch personnel is substantially conditioned by the laws governing the various classified services—military, foreign, and civil. In laws determining pay, promotion schedules, bargaining rights of employees, fringe benefits, grievance procedures, special allowances, leaves and sickness regulations, removal charges, etc., Congress can mightily influence personnel practices and agency morale in the entire federal service. It can also confound and limit the ability of top federal executives, including the President, to develop flexible and efficient management practices. There is always tension between the President and parts of the Congress as to who shall control the bureaucracy. One force on the legislative side is the recognition by departments, agencies, and bureaus that committees like Armed Services, Foreign Relations (Foreign Affairs in the House), and Post Office and Civil Service, *and* their subcommittee counterparts on Appropriations, have vast powers over the several classified services. Agency loyalty to the President wears thin in competition with subunits of Congress powerfully situated and powerfully vested to affect pay, promotions, and perquisites of federal employees.

Indirect Pressures

Beyond confirmation and laws governing the classified services, there has been since the beginning of the Republic a no man's land of indirect congressional influence over executive branch personnel, high and low. Until President Nixon's historic "bite the bullet" speech to the press of February 5, 1969, most postmasters had for almost 200 years been subject to patronage appointments involving congressional clearances. Over the years, throughout the federal service, many officials have been shifted, chastened, withdrawn from consideration, or otherwise influenced as a result of quiet words passed by powerful committee chairmen, or as a result of oblique sentences in committee or subcommittee reports. These indirect pressures are sometimes highly, sometimes lowly, motivated. But in every case they are manifestations of the exercise of pluralistic power in the Congress and in the government as a whole. They are the often tarnished hallmarks of a system of dispersed sovereignty.

Oversight by Direct Organizational and Policy Controls

No department or agency is created without an act of Congress. And since changes in structure can often affect the direction of policy and the weight of authority, Congress insists upon a direct voice in schemes for reorganizing the executive branch. This it does through the "legislative veto." A reorganization plan submitted by the President may take effect after ninety days unless during that period one or both houses of Congress have voted against the plan. How seriously the power centers in Congress view matters of executive branch organization may be judged from the fact that since World War II nearly a third of the President's reorganization plans have been defeated. The President may see reorganization plans in terms of efficiency and coordination in the executive branch. Powerfully situated congressmen, however, may see in the same plans a dilution of their direct influence over a particular agency or bureau, a decrease in the executive unit's sensitivity to particular outside interests, or a lessening of the autonomy of a "friendly" bureau which does not wish to be "coordinated."

It is the considered judgment of some of America's most knowledgeable students of the federal government that further attempts to make the executive branch more efficient by structural reorganization will not be successful until either the jurisdictional jealousies of congressional committees are weakened or the committee jurisdictions themselves are reorganized. From the standpoint of functional coordination and intelligent policy planning, for example, it might make considerable sense to amalgamate the Department of Agriculture and the Department of the Interior into a single Department of Natural Resources. This will not soon happen. Departmental resistance would be mild compared to the resistance of those congressmen who would find their present pattern of power over one of these two departments (or some units thereof) disrupted or destroyed.

Beyond organizational questions, Congress takes a direct interest in executive branch policies. Congressional laws, of course, establish the business of executive agencies. These general policy guides necessarily permit substantial executive discretion. In certain fields, especially where the political interests of congressmen might be directly affected (e.g., the location or discontinuation of military bases), legislative attempts to limit executive discretion are common. These limitations may appear as language in appropriations subcommittee reports; as concurrent resolutions giving the sense of Congress (e.g., against the recognition of Communist China); as statutory requirements that certain agency policies may not take effect until they have been cleared with a congressional committee, or until a report has been before Congress for a certain period of time. Some of these devices, especially committee clearance, are sufficiently disruptive of executive branch efficiency and responsibility that they are now being systematically vetoed by the President. In the first session of the 89th Congress, President Johnson vetoed two major bills on the grounds of an unconstitutional invasion of executive branch discretion by subunits of Congress.

The Congressional Dilemma

Congress is still trying to find an appropriate role as watch dog and hound dog. The dilemmas are unsettling. On the one hand, it is clear that somewhere in this area of investigation and administrative oversight lie some of Congress' most important functions. One does not have to become an uncritical follower of Max Weber to appreciate the dangers to society of an unchecked bureaucracy. Potentially, congressional committees are allies of the President in holding executive branch managers and technicians politically accountable. Furthermore, many social evils need exposure through public investigations. With the power of subpoena, and with certain procedural flexibilities, Congress can go further in exposing social evils than can the press or the courts.

And yet Congress must necessarily delegate its hound dog and watch dog functions to individuals in committee. This means all too frequently that personal and parochial interests are built into the calculus of operations which ideally should enjoy a high degree of disinterestedness.

Congress itself has been aware of this dilemma. That is why its investigatory and oversight functions are presently divided among (1) substantive committees with surveillance responsibilities over relevant executive agencies; (2) appropriations subcommittees; (3) either select or standing committees with special or general mandates to conduct investigations or to oversee the executive. Contemporary or recent examples of the third category include: the two Committees on Government Operations, the Senate Special Committee on Aging, the House Committee on Internal Security, the two Committees on Small Business, the House Select Committee on Government Research, and the Joint Committee on Reduction of Non-Essential Federal Expenditures.

Even with this crosshatching of committee jurisdictions, the problem remains how to maintain a healthy surveillance of bureaucratic and societal performance without infusing controls and influences that are even more parochial and disutile than the evils exposed.

The Joint Committee on the Organization of Congress in the spring and summer of 1965 viewed a number of suggestions for improving oversight and investigatory functions. Included were proposals to create a series of permanent joint study committees for continuing critical scrutiny of existing programs; establish a congressional scientific advisory and research agency; establish an oversight subcommittee for each substantive committee; set up an "Ombudsman" to investigate constituent claims of bureaucratic officiousness or ineptitude; adopt wider committee use of question-review sessions with agency officials; and other related reforms.[9]

Until these or other suggestions turn out to be practical, the nation must settle for the healthy impact upon the executive branch and the society as a whole of the *right* of Congress to investigate and to oversee. The nation must also settle for the fact that the exercise of this important legislative prerogative is in practice intermittent, sometimes indifferent in quality, and frequently parochial.

Chapter VIII

TOWARD A MORE RESPONSIBLE CONGRESS

Responsibility is an ambiguous word. It may refer to the ethical behavior of individuals. It may refer to the collective behavior and accountability of a group or institution.

In this final chapter, we shall take a brief look at both contexts: responsibility in terms of ethical standards for individuals in Congress; responsibility in terms of norms for the legislative branch as a whole.

CONGRESSIONAL ETHICS

In a tribute to Congress in June 1965, former Vice President Hubert H. Humphrey said in part, "I have seen in the Halls of Congress more idealism, more humaneness, more compassion, more profiles of courage than in any other institution that I have ever known."[1] A decade and a half earlier, a U. S. senator who had spent most of his life as a successful businessman said, "I have seen more [moral courage] in a day here in the Senate than the average businessman sees in a year, or even in a lifetime."[2]

Discounting the biases of club loyalty, these words of praise are reminders that the personal and public ethics of congressmen are far higher than cynics avow or than intermittent scandals in the press suggest. Like any other sampling of human beings, Congress has a few whose sense of probity is egregiously elastic. Like most social systems, Congress suffers from internal deferences and loyalties which are at times overly protective of wrongdoing. Like many professions (e.g., medicine, law, the ministry, business) politics sets or adjusts to standards of conduct that are internally comfortable and personally supportive even when they are socially harmful and/or ethically questionable. But faced with a myriad of temptations of power and money, congressmen by and large maintain high standards of personal and group conduct.

There are, however, two ethical jungles which need clearing: campaign finance and conflict of interest. Both areas are amenable to substantial improvement by adjustments in existing laws and by the establishment of adequate ethical-practices review systems. In truth, some limited progress has been made in the latter field within the past few years. But much remains to be done, and in the meantime Congress will bear a heavy, corrosive, and unnecessary burden of public suspicion and disapprobation, and in the case of campaign expenditures, will commit itself to a continuation of practices which violate the spirit if not the letter of the law.

A useful setting for a discussion of these issues may be found in the so-called "Bobby Baker investigations" held in the early 1960's. That case brought to light such a variety of questionable practices rooted in legislative influence that it furnishes a prototype of contemporary congressional practices needing correction. It also, by implication, indicates the major lines of essential reform.

Even an examination of the cast of characters is instructive. It included: (1) legislators and their powerfully situated assistants; (2) men identified with the money-raising end of political campaigns; (3) lobbyists acting as brokers between the buyers and sellers of influence; (4) outside interests and individuals standing to gain from association and affiliation with influence peddlers; (5) officials, public and private, whose discretionary judgment can grant or withhold things of value (licenses, loans, contracts, jobs, etc.). These were the interlocking roles played in the Bobby Baker drama. In a generic sense, it has ever been so.

Bobby Baker's Power

Bobby Baker's power derived from three sources: (1) his long and intimate knowledge of the Senate and of powerfully situated senators; (2) his position as Secretary of the Senate Majority; and (3) his position as Secretary-Treasurer of the Senate Democratic Campaign Committee. A word needs to be said about each of these.

He had first come to the Senate as a page at the age of 14. His talents of affability and shrewdness made him chief Democratic page at 16, chief of the Democratic cloakroom at 18, and secretary of the Democratic minority at 24. At 26, in 1955, he became secretary to the Democratic majority. Close to page-boy and cloakroom gossip for years, Baker absorbed a vast fund of information about the powerful men he observed. He came to know deference patterns and channels of influence. And he came to understand the horse trades of mutuality, compromise, and logrolling that at their best are the salvation of a free society, but at their worst are sinister and self-seeking.

To this knowledge of backstairs gossip Baker added an understanding of the substance and procedures of Senate business. After all, this was his business as clerk of the Democratic cloakroom and later secretary of the Democratic minority and then majority. In this latter role he knew what bills were coming up on the floor and whether a particular senator's vote was needed. In the case of a senator's absence he arranged voting pairs, and usually he knew how individual senators would line up on any issue. On important roll calls he was available at the entrance to the floor of the Senate to give the majority leader's position. And on a host of matters, like office space, private bills, supplies, committee assignments, living quarters, or internal patronage, if Baker couldn't arrange matters, he knew who could.

The final ingredient in Baker's power came from his work for the Senate Democratic Campaign Committee. Here he was introduced to the realities of party finance; the expectations of large givers; the enormous return on investments supported by political influence; the availability of "credit" to those with proper connections.

With his intimate knowledge of the Senate, the string of indebtednesses owed him for favors rendered as secretary of the Senate majority, and his knowledge of the odorous financial fringe to the garment of politics, Baker parlayed his modest Senate salary into a $2,000,000 fortune.

Bobby Baker's Activities

A brief look at a few of the dozen or so cases investigated by the Senate Committee on Rules and Administration in 1964 and 1965 yields some interesting lessons.[3]

Bobby Baker's activities came into the open as a result of the "Vending Contracts Case," a civil suit in which a former business associate charged that Baker had used influence to obtain contracts for Serv-U-Corp (a company in which Baker owned a substantial interest) in certain defense plants. The fact that there was no public registry of Senate employees' financial holdings or business associations had allowed Baker to function without the vigilant attention of members of the opposition party or of a sniffing and hungry press. Without the fortuitous circumstance of a private lawsuit, Baker's activities might have continued unnoticed.

The "Case of the D. C. Stadium" involved an insurance associate of Baker, Don B. Reynolds, who testified that Baker had helped him to secure a performance bond for a construction firm, in return for which Reynolds paid $4,000 (of the $10,000 commission) to Baker and $1,500 to the clerk of the House District of Columbia Committee. In addition, it was alleged that Baker had conspired with the contractor for the stadium, who happened to be Matthew McCloskey, treasurer of the Democratic National Committee, to make a sizable overpayment to Reynolds, of which $25,000 would be siphoned off for the 1960 Democratic presidential campaign. Whether true or not, the testimony sketches a prototype of the symbiosis that links part of the construction industry to political influence via campaign contributions and personal pay-offs. No series of reforms can break entirely this kind of conspiracy. But changes in the methods of raising and reporting campaign money, and the proposed requirement of disclosure mentioned above, would go a long way toward improving the moral climate of American politics.

The "Case of the Freight Forwarders" concerned a lobbyist who, after successful passage of a bill favoring his clients, paid $5,000 to Baker's law partner. The latter deposited the check and wrote Baker another check for the same amount. The lobbyist testified that the payment to Baker was made for services unrelated to the passage of the bill. Here we see the outlines of perhaps the most widespread abuse of ethical standards: the practice of allowing one's law firm to benefit improperly from the office one holds. Congress has not even begun the process of sorting out effective bench marks to guide sound judgments in this area of ethical concern.

Another case involved the purchase of stock by Baker (through loans arranged for him by lobbyists) in a company whose value multiplied many times after a favorable tax ruling was secured from the Internal Revenue Service reportedly at the intervention of a congressman. Here again conflict of interest was the underlying issue.

In some ways the ethical lapses of Baker are less disturbing than the reaction of other senators to such deviations. At one point in the investigation when a transaction involving Senator George A. Smathers (D., Florida) was being discussed, Chairman B. Everett Jordan (D., North Carolina) was asked if Smathers would be called to testify. "We're not investigating Senators," replied the Chairman—leaving the problem of who will investigate senators if other senators will not. Perhaps the unhappiest aspect of the whole Bobby Baker episode was the sense conveyed to the public that the committee was attempting to cover up a situation which might be embarrassing to many influential people.

Limited Reform: Conflicts of Interest

Largely as a result of the Bobby Baker case, the Senate in 1964 created a bipartisan Select Committee on Standards and Conduct. After the disclosures of various financial improprieties by Senator Thomas J. Dodd (D., Connecticut) and Representative Adam Clayton Powell (D., New York) in 1967, the House followed the Senate's example. In 1968 it created a new standing committee on Standards and Official Conduct.

More important, as a result of the Baker, Dodd, and Powell episodes, both houses in 1968 passed resolutions setting forth rules and codes of official conduct for themselves and employees, and they passed resolutions that for the first time in history required senators and representatives to make at least limited financial-disclosure reports. Some financial data was to be made public; more detailed disclosures were to be filed in sealed envelopes with the understanding that they could be opened only by a majority vote of the House Committee on Standards of Official Conduct or the Senate Committee on Standards and Conduct respectively.

Unfortunately for public confidence, enormous loopholes were permitted in the disclosure resolutions in both houses. One example from many: 80 members of the House are lawyers. They were not directed by the disclosure resolution to list the names of clients. In short, if a step in the right direction has been taken, a hundred steps are needed before the public will have the assurance that Congress is willing to police itself on issues of conflict of interest—of making personal financial gain from the holding of public office.

No Reform: Campaign Finance Laws

A number of federal statutes govern campaign finance, notably the Corrupt Practices Act of 1925, imposing limits on campaign expenditures, and the 1940 amendments to the Hatch Act, imposing limits on contributions. Additional laws prohibit both unions and corporations from donating money in connection with federal elections.

But the reporting requirements are unaccompanied by enforcement provisions and the intent of these laws is so easy to evade that they have been conspicuously ineffective. The Hatch Act, for example, sets a $5,000 annual limit on an individual's contributions to any candidate or committee, but it says nothing to prohibit every member of a large, wealthy family from contributing individually; nor does it preclude the formation of several committees for a particular candidate, to each of which an individual may contribute $5,000.

On the expenditure side, restrictions are equally meaningless, applying only to monies spent or services rendered by others on the candidate's behalf. Furthermore, restrictions do not apply to primaries.

In recent years, suggestions for reform have come principally through studies made in 1956 and 1957 by the Privileges and Elections Subcommittee of the Senate Rules and Administration Committee; through the scholarly works of Alexander Heard and Herbert Alexander;[4] and through President Kennedy's Commission on Campaign Costs. Perhaps the most systematic proposals have come from the Commission.

The major findings and recommendations of these efforts found their way into a comprehensive message on campaign financing submitted by President Johnson to Congress in May 1967. The Johnson program aimed at five goals:

1. to assure full disclosure of contributions and expenses, to place realistic limitations on contributions, and to remove meaningless and ineffective ceilings on campaign expenditures;
2. to provide a system of public financing for presidential election campaigns;
3. to broaden the base of public support for election campaigns by exploring ways to encourage and stimulate small contributions;
4. to close loopholes in the Federal laws regulating lobbying;
5. to assure the right to vote for millions of Americans who change their residences.

Implementing bills were introduced into the Congress in 1967 and again in 1968. A modified version of a part of the Johnson proposal was submitted to the 91st Congress (1969) by outgoing Attorney General Ramsey Clark. As of this writing, however, Congress has found it impossible to pass a campaign finance reform measure.

The unwillingness of Congress to clean house is discouraging. Perhaps there is a feeling that the present patterns of campaign finance insure a kind of functional representation that reflects the interests of major economic groups in our society, and that such representation is needed to offset alleged popular passions.

Whatever the reasons, excuses, or justification for inaction on revising laws governing campaign costs and conflicts of interest, Congress pays a heavy price in increased public cynicism. Moral courage and high ethical practice exist in Congress. Careful students of Congress believe this to be the rule rather than the exception. Politics ennobles more than it corrupts. If higher ethical standards are demanded of political figures than of others, it is right that this be so, for politicians are the people's guardians quite as much as vice versa. The fact is, however, that the ethical reality is lower than it should be.

Public cynicism is not friendly to freedom. If Congress is to retain a position of strength in our federal system, it must retain the public's confidence. The public's confidence cannot be retained over time if the congressional image is tarnished by the misdeeds of a few, or by laws and practices that patently encourage law-breaking and inequities in political and economic advantage in our society.

The problems of congressional ethics, of course, go far beyond conflict of interest and campaign costs. But these are central. They are what lead to the more egregious examples of "sub-governments" and special privilege noted in earlier chapters.

TOWARD A MORE RESPONSIBLE CONGRESS

The United States enters the last third of the twentieth century as the most powerful nation on earth. Its military strength and its diplomatic and economic resources affect the lives and fortunes of the entire human race. Its perceived national interests lead it into infusive influences upon stability and change in scores of nations across the face of the globe. At home, the American government has become a major agent of economic growth and stability, of social amelioration, of cultural and educational adaptation and initiative, of scientific and technological advance.

It has been forced into these various responsibilities—domestic and international—by human interdependencies produced by technology and urbanization, and by the values and expectations of the preamble to its Constitution. The burden of government has never been more complex, the need for responsible and effective instruments of government never more insistent.

Does the picture of Congress which emerges from the preceding chapters give us confidence that our national legislature is effectively organized for what Herbert Agar once called "a time for greatness"?

Four measures of performance suggest themselves:

1. Do present relations between the Congress and the executive branch provide responsible and rational answers to pressing national and international needs; and is each house politically accountable in the sense of having a visible partisan majority that controls organization and procedures and at the same time serves as a base for a responsible coalition on matters of substance?

2. Are sources of power in the Congress sufficiently independent to insure a critical and constructive review of presidential proposals and of bureaucratic performance, while at the same time they are not overly reflective of special and parochial interests?

3. Is the membership of the House of Representatives truly consonant with the Constitutional mandate for equality of representation?

4. Is the internal machinery of Congress sufficiently and rationally organized to provide an effective balance between deliberation and dispatch in handling the nation's business?

The only fair answer is that the new Congress represents progress on all of these fronts—but that there is still substantial room for improvement.

Executive-Legislative Relations and Party Responsibility

During nine out of the ten years that marked the decade of the 1960's, a majority in both houses of Congress, as well as the President, were of the same political party. It is fair to say that of the four relevant Congresses (87th, 88th, 89th, and 90th), a benign coalition dominated only the 89th. It will be remembered that a benign coalition was earlier defined as one in which the coalition voting on any particular issue is based on a majority from the party that has organized the Congress, or one house thereof. In terms of the capacity of the public to hold elected representatives accountable for policy choices (one of the fundamental philosophical tenets of democracy), a kind of triple benignity occurs when the President, a majority in the Senate, a majority in the House of Representatives are of the same party and policy persuasion.

The first session of the 89th Congress, which ended October 23, 1965, was the most dramatic illustration in a generation of the capacity of the President and the Congress to work together on important issues of public policy. In part a mopping up operation on an agenda fashioned at least in spirit by the New Deal, the work of the 89th Congress cut new paths through the frontier of qualitative issues: a beautification bill, a bill to create federal support for the arts and humanities, vast increases in federal aid to education. Both parties (in retrospect too uncritically) supported presidential requests in the field of national security policy. In any case, the policy leadership and the legislative skill of President Johnson found a ready and supportive response from a strengthened partisan leadership and a substantial, presidentially oriented Democratic majority in both houses. A decade of incremental structural changes in the locus of power in both houses eased the President's task of consent-building and of legislative implementation.

Yet Congress was far from being just a rubber stamp. On some issues the President met resounding defeat. On many issues, presidential recommendations were modified by excisions or additions—reflecting the power of particular committee chairmen, group interests, and bureaucratic pressures at odds with presidential perspectives.

One glaring deficiency emerged in the legislative output of the 89th Congress: lack of adequate attention to the *administrative* implications of the new domestic legislation. Laws were passed without appropriate questions being asked about the availability of trained manpower to carry out the programs; about optimum relationships between and among federal, state, local, and private implementing agencies; or about the effective interdepartmental coordination of old and new activities. Often it is too late to handle such questions by *post hoc* accounting and surveillance procedures. Part of the slowness in fashioning President Nixon's legislative program can be attributed to his recognition that bold new programs inadequately administered and funded can be a political liability.

Overall, however, the lessons of the 89th Congress were positive. It proved that vigorous presidential leadership and sizable partisan majorities in both houses of the same partisan persuasion as the President, could act in reasonable consonance, and with dispatch, in fashioning creative answers to major problems. The nation's voters could pin responsibility upon a national party for the legislative output. If that partisan majority erred in judgment, it could at least be held accountable in ensuing congressional and presidential elections.

The unhappy reality is that the 89th Congress was an abberation from a less harmonious norm. For most of the decade, under Presidents Kennedy, Johnson, and Nixon, some form of inverted coalition slowed, substantially modified, or blocked key elements of the legislative programs submitted by the nation's chief executive. And, of course, a partisan division between the two houses of Congress, on the one hand, and the President, on the other, is a reality as the nation enters the decade of the 1970's.

If the political kaleidoscope continues in Washington, it is nonetheless encouraging and clear that traditional forces of social and economic reaction in the Congress, regardless of party, are far weaker than they were when the decade of the '60's began. Furthermore, reapportionment, new racial mixtures in suburbia as well as in central-city peripheries, and economic pluralism are producing an increasing consistency between congressional and presidential views of the national interest. Even with divided partisanship, therefore, the President and the Congress should face, in the years ahead, fewer unresolvable confrontations than in the decades behind us.

Actually, the areas of greatest tension and conflict are likely to occur not between the President and partisan leadership in both houses. The dangerous conflicts will be between the President and his partisan congressional leaders on the one hand, and executive-bureau/congressional-committee/interest-group coalitions on the other. This is the long engagement between the king and the barons which has given drama to so much of human history. Total victory for either side can produce either tyranny or a dangerous fragmentation of power. Tension between the two forces—with an edge to the king—is probably the key to achieving national purpose without loss of freedom.

The present balance is, however, sufficiently precarious to suggest that further measures are in order to strengthen centripetal forces within each house. The twin principles of seniority and committee autonomy—substantially weakened in the past decade—need to be modified even further. Majority membership controls within committees need to be increased vis-à-vis the power of committee chairmen. Majorities in each party in both houses need to develop more effective controls over their own caucuses, and through their leadership and their representative policy committees, more effective influence over committee assignments and floor calendars. If these oblique attacks prove to be inadequate, the evils of seniority may have to be attacked head on. But there is evidence to suggest that some of the advantages of seniority can be continued while conditions can be set to limit the more egregious manifestations of the practice.

Centripetal forces will be further strengthened by additional symbiotic linkages between the campaign committees in the Congress and the national committees of the two major parties.

Finally, the energy, skill, and understanding of the President will be a major factor in strengthening party leadership in each house. In the modern world, no parliament can function effectively without strong and continuing executive leadership.

Legislative Review and the Oversight of Administration

When one turns from general directions of public policy, and partisan responsibility for general legislative output, to questions of legislative detail and administrative surveillance, the new Congress deserves lower marks. Parochialisms abound. Congress lacks adequate counterparts to the moralizing and rational forces of hierarchy in the executive branch. The presidential perspective may be wrong, but it is fashioned by the need to place a series of countervailing and parochial interests in the society and in the bureaucracy into some kind of general framework related to a national electoral majority. In the Congress, the unified programs of the President's State of the Union message, budget, and economic report are carved up into separate subcommittee and committee referrals and analyses. Too often bills are marked up by parochial pens. Too often patterns of internal deference in Congress lead to full committee and floor acceptance of myopic subcommittee amendments. Too often seniority gives undue personal, area, or functional advantage to a small number of powerfully situated legislators. The ideal editing of major legislative issues is not likely to come from compromises between general and parochial views. It should come—at least in part—from a compromise between two competing views of the general interest. The latter cannot be achieved by destroying the division of labor within the Congress. It can only be achieved by:

——promoting to positions of responsibility in the committee system what Mazzini once called "the best and the wisest" rather than merely the oldest in the Congress;

——periodically reorganizing the committee and subcommittee

structure of Congress to eliminate outmoded and limited jurisdictional interests;

——improving internal intercommittee communications within the Congress—perhaps by establishing one or two crosscutting committees for a general review of the President's program (e.g., a Joint Committee on the Budget; a Joint Committee on the State of the Union);

——continuing to strengthen the power of the staff of party leaders in both houses; and

——improving the quality but not necessarily the quantity of staff aides to individual congressional committees, and using university and other external professional consultants far more extensively.

The Joint Committee on the Organization of the Congress addressed itself to many of these issues in 1965. Unfortunately, in the years since, Congress has not acted on the most important of the Joint Committee's recommendations.

The same therapy is called for in administrative surveillance. Whether surveillance takes place through advice and consent, through appropriations subcommittee hearings, through substantive committee hearings and investigations, or through control over executive branch organization, means must be found within the Congress to broaden the perspective of nearsighted wielders of parochial power. Politicians become statesmen as they are induced to react to more inclusive interests. Scattered power can be constructive if the vision and the accountability of each power-holder is broadly gauged and broadly based. Whatever reforms of politics or congressional organization move in this direction will tend to promote the public interest.

Perhaps the area in which Congress needs most general improvement in deliberation is foreign affairs. The American people need the advantage of intelligent congressional debates over major foreign policy issues. Deferring to the President on many national security issues is inevitable and prudent. But Congress needs to do far more than this. It needs to serve as a forum for informed discussion about such long-range issues as our relations with China; the future of nonwhites and whites in Southern Africa; the successes and failures of our Latin American policies; the development of the United Nations system into a more effective world government. Individual speeches are not enough, no matter how brave or eloquent. Committee hearings and the floor of each house should be used far more extensively for general debates on foreign policy. Surely there are other options available to the Congress in its relations with the executive in foreign affairs than blind deference on the one hand or irresponsible, boat-rocking attack on the other. America's national interest is best served in foreign affairs when Presidents act prudently within a matrix of continuing questioning and concern evinced by the Congress, and when Congress itself helps to foment useful colloquies about long-range alternatives and goals.

The Representativeness of the House

The struggle for equal representation among congressional districts has been all but won, although individual battles are still going on. By 1972 after redistricting that will follow the decennial census of 1970, the grossest illustrations of malapportionment will have been finally corrected. Minor distortions will continue to exist through the practice of gerrymandering—giving undue advantage to a party or to an ideology or interest. But recent Supreme Court decisions are forcing, and will continue to force, an equitable correspondence between population and representation in the House of Representatives.

Since suburbia will profit more than central cities from reapportionment, the effect of the *Wesberry, Kirkpatrick,* and *Wells* cases will be to strengthen the power of suburban interests and viewpoints in the society as a whole. Whether this will be at the expense of the poor and minority groups in the central cities will not depend solely upon the capacity of the President, party, education, civic leadership, and religion to broaden man's sense of community and social responsibility—important as these forces can and will be. Inexorable demographic shifts are making an increasing number of suburbs subject to the same racial and economic tensions that until recently have been associated only with central cities. As this change accelerates, legislators will find identities of interest between those (Black and white) in poverty (a diminishing number) and those in a hard-pressed lower-middle class (an increasing number). Sorting out these new pressures and new claims within a context of continuing racial tensions and fiscal stringencies will not be easy. But as Carl Rogers has written, the ability of Western democratic cultures "to respond appropriately—at the last, cliff-hanging moment—to those trends which challenge their survival" is impressive. And a younger and extraordinarily vocal generation is coming of age determined to solve the race problem in this nation sooner rather than later.

And there are political forces moving in the same direction.The Voting Rights Acts of 1965 and 1968 will insure that American Blacks in both the North and the South will increase their political bargaining power. But, by itself, this power (except in isolated instances) is limited. The logic of American politics has always been for minorities—even antagonistic ones—to coalesce around goals that are commonly held. It is highly probable that economic interests will be more powerful than racial bigotry in dictating the future of American politics.

The Machinery of Congress

Finally, if Congress is to become a more responsible instrument of the public interest, both houses need to improve their internal machinery. As a functioning organism, Congress is woefully arthritic. In a study made by Arthur D. Little, Inc., leading management consultants, for the NBC News in 1965, the conclusion was reached that Congress is "so overloaded with work it is not staffed or equipped to handle that it cannot function effectively in the twentieth century."[5] The Little study contrasts the methods congressmen must use with those used by such giant corporations as du Pont, "where accurate information on almost any subject relating to the company's activities is available through the use of computers and other electronic devices."[6]

It is of course fatuous to measure congressional organization and performance solely against the patterns of giant industry. Congress cannot mount either the internal sanctions or the clarity of goals of great private corporations. But Congress can and should borrow some of the techniques of efficient management from both public and private organizations. This need is especially valid in information retrieval, payroll practices, personnel management, communications systems, central housekeeping, clerical and mail services, and program evaluation and review. Management sciences have improved radically in recent years. Some improvements are not transferable to Congress without subverting basic legislative functions or prerogatives (e.g., in-house testing and measurement of individuals). But many management techniques and certain types of electronic hardware could undoubtedly improve the efficiency of congressional operations.

Certainly one field for rich exploration is the committee system itself. An increase in joint hearings—within each house and between each house—could save executive as well as congressional time. A central clearing house to help avoid conflicts in scheduling committee and subcommittee meetings would diminish frustration and increase the orderliness of conducting legislative business. Further encouragement of advance testimony with appropriate abstracts would cut the time of, and increase the quality of deliberation in, congressional hearings.

Floor procedures are in even greater need of attention. Traditional rules, or interpretations thereof, governing the reading of the *Journal*, quorum calls, unanimous consent, germaneness, cloture, and roll calls need critical review and amendment. Some procedural delays promote desirable deliberation. But many are anachronisms—the residue of a distant past or of unconscionable minority interests. The business of Congress is too massive in quantity and too important in quality to permit uncritically accepted tradition or precedent to govern the conduct of legislative business on the floor.

Only Congress itself, of course, can work out realistic and acceptable guidelines for improving its performance. One mark of the new Congress is a visible concern with finding an appropriate role in the American government system and with discovering rules and procedures which will make its new role possible and viable. But in this search the Congress must have the sympathetic assistance of the President, the party system, the press, the universities, and the concerned electorate. For Congress is an integral part of a larger society. In the words of Alfred North Whitehead, "those societies which cannot combine reverence to their symbols with freedom of revision, must ultimately decay from anarchy or from the slow atrophy of a life stifled by useless shadows."[7]

Congress and Freedom

For all of its weaknesses and inadequacies, Congress is a major bastion of human freedom. This point would hardly need elaboration were it not so frequently and tragically forgotten in the mid-twentieth century.

If anything is clear in this fretful age, it is that legislative institutions which gave freedom its birth and meaning have been eroded in power and denigrated in reputation the world around—eroded and denigrated, that is, where they have not been totally destroyed. Necessary as the Gaullist revolution in France may have been, nobody will pretend that the French National Assembly was upgraded in power or influence by the change. The first casualty of wobbly novitiates in the family of nations seems to be their parliaments or assemblies. In the past few years, a half-dozen new nations have abolished the pretense of democracy, and have reverted to rule by tribal chieftains decked out in modern military garb. Scrawled in invisible ink on the walls of the empty parliament buildings are the words, "Parliaments, Go Home."

How short historical memories are! It was a congress of nobles that met at Runnymede to make John Lackland sign the Magna Carta. It was a congress of estates called "Parliament" that gradually reduced the prerogatives of the English crown from absolutism to a benign symbol of spiritual and moral unity. It was assemblies of free men which tempered and hamstrung the insolence of appointed royal governors during our own colonial days.

Of what does freedom consist, unless it is the atmosphere of human dignity made possible by the existence of representative restraints upon rulers? Benevolent despots have dotted the pages of human history, but no one knows when a despot is going to stop being benevolent. And on this score, history is not encouraging.

It was with considerations of this sort in mind that our Founding Fathers, after a brief preamble, began the Constitution of the United

States with the words, "All legislative Powers herein granted shall be vested in a Congress of the United States, which shall consist of a Senate and House of Representatives."

That the first article of the Constitution deals with the Congress is no accident. Congress is first because, living in the long shadow of the Glorious Revolution of 1688 and of its great philosophical defender, John Locke, the Founding Fathers fully understood that although you could have government without a representative assembly, you could not have *free* government without a representative assembly.

Congress defends freedom by asking rude questions; by stubbornly insisting that technology be discussed in terms of its human effects; by eliciting new ideas from old heads; by building a sympathetic bridge between the bewildered citizen and the bureaucracy; by acting as a sensitive register for group interests whose fortunes are indistinguishable from the fortunes of vast numbers of citizens and who have a constitutional right to be heard.

Congress defends freedom by being a prudent provider; by carefully sifting and refining legislative proposals; by compromising and homogenizing raw forces in conflict; by humbling generals and admirals —and, on occasion, even Presidents.

For as far ahead as man can see, freedom is an eternal frontier. If not constantly cleared and defended it reverts to jungle where wild beasts play out their morbid and sullen dramas. As one of the great institutional forces in the life of modern man dedicated to the perpetuation of freedom, Congress in the last analysis deserves our respect and our reverence.[8]

Notes

CHAPTER I

1. Alexander Hamilton, John Jay, and James Madison, *The Federalist* (New York: Willey Book Company, 1901), Paper No. LI, p. 290.
2. Westberry et al v. Sanders, 376 U.S. 1 (1964); Kirkpatrick v. Preisler; Wells v. Rockefeller.
3. H. Douglas Price, "The Electoral Arena," in David B. Truman (ed.), *The Congress and America's Future,* The American Assembly, Columbia University (Englewood Cliffs: Prentice-Hall, 1965), p. 33.
4. *New York Times,* August 25, 1965, p. 48.
5. Charles L. Clapp, *The Congressman: His Work as He Sees It* (Washington, D.C.: Brookings Institution, 1963), p. 331.
6. *Ibid.,* p. 332.
7. *Ibid.*
8. (Englewood Cliffs, N.J.: Prentice-Hall Inc., 1966).
9. See Warren Miller and Donald Stokes, "Party Government and the Saliency of Congress," *Public Opinion Quarterly,* XXVI (Winter 1962), pp. 531-546.
10. Warren Miller and Donald Stokes, *Representation in Congress, op. cit.*

CHAPTER II

1. Earl Latham, "Interest Groups in the American Political System," in Stephen K. Bailey (ed.) *American Politics and Government: Essays in Essentials,* (New York: Basic Books, 1965), p. 148.
2. Alexander Hamilton, John Jay, and James Madison, *The Federalist* (New York: Willey Book Company, 1901), Paper No. X, p. 46.
3. Stephen K. Bailey, "Lobbying," *Encyclopaedia Britannica,* Vol. 14 (1963), pp. 259-260.
4. Pendleton Herring, *Group Representation Before Congress,* (Baltimore: Johns Hopkins Press, 1929), p. 237.
5. See Roscoe C. Martin, *The Cities and the Federal System* (New York: Atherton Press, 1965), p. 175.
6. *Congressional Quarterly Weekly Report,* Vol. XXVII, No. 26 (Washington D.C.: Congressional Quarterly Inc., June 27, 1969), p. 1130.
7. See Raymond A. Bauer, Ithiel de Sola Pool and Lewis Anthony Dexter, *American Business and Public Policy: The Politics of Foreign Trade* (New York: Atherton Press, 1963), *passim.*
8. Lester Milbrath, "Lobbying as a Communication Process," *Public Opinion Quarterly,* Spring 1960, as quoted in Douglass Cater, *Power in Washington* (New York: Random House, 1964), p. 209.

9. See Stanley Kelley, Jr., *Professional Public Relations and Political Power* (Baltimore: Johns Hopkins Press, 1956), Chapter II.
10. Charles L. Clapp, *The Congressman: His Work as He Sees It* (Washington: Brookings Institution, 1963), pp. 371-2.
11. See Douglass Cater, *op. cit.*
12. See Philip M. Stern, *The Great Treasury Raid* (New York: Random House, 1964).

CHAPTER III

1. Richard E. Neustadt, "Planning the President's Program," in Theodore J. Lowi (ed.), *Legislative Politics, U.S.A.*, 2nd Ed. (Boston: Little Brown and Company, 1965), pp. 123-4.
2. Warren Miller and Donald Stokes, "Constituency Influence in Congress," *American Political Science Review,* LVII (March 1963), pp. 45-56.
3. *New York Times,* July 13, 1965, p. 22.

CHAPTER IV

1. Richard F. Fenno, Jr., "The Internal Distribution of Influence: The House," in David B. Truman (ed.), *The Congress and America's Future,* The American Assembly, Columbia University, (Englewood Cliffs, N.J.: Prentice-Hall, 1965), p. 59.
2. *Ibid.*
3. Ralph K. Huitt, "The Internal Distribution of Influence: The Senate," in David B. Truman (ed.), *op. cit.*, p. 80.
4. See Joseph S. Clark and other Senators, *The Senate Establishment* (New York: Hill and Wang, 1963), pp. 10-15.
5. Richard Bolling, *House Out of Order* (New York: E. P. Dutton & Co., 1965), p. 210.
6. See H.R.8, 89th Cong. 1st Sess.
7. Daniel M. Berman, *In Congress Assembled* (New York: Macmillan Company, 1964), pp. 230-1.

CHAPTER V

1. See Gilbert Y. Steiner, *The Congressional Conference Committee* (Urbana: University of Illinois Press, 1951).
2. See Richard F. Fenno, Jr., "The House Appropriations Committee in a Political System: The Problem of Integration," *The American Political Science Review,* LVI, June 1962, pp. 310-324.
3. *Congressional Reform,* (Washington, D.C.: Congressional Quarterly, Inc. Special Report Revised April 1964), p. 18.
4. Dean Acheson, *A Citizen Looks at Congress* (New York: Harper and Row, 1956), pp. 122-23.
5. See Douglass Cater, *Power in Washington* (New York: Random House, 1964), Ch. 2.

CHAPTER VI

For the tale of events analyzed in this chapter, I am heavily indebted to the research of Howard E. Schuman, Daniel M. Berman, H. Douglas Price, the Congressional Quarterly Service, and the *New York Times.* I am especially grateful for the research and some of the wording in this chapter prepared by Joul S. Berke.

1. *New York Times,* August 17, 1969, p. 42.
2. Howard E. Schuman, "Senate Rules and the Civil Rights Bill: A Case Study," in Theodore J. Lowi (ed.), *Legislative Politics, USA,* 2nd ed., (Boston: Little, Brown and Company, 1965), pp. 32-33.
3. *Ibid.*, pp. 42-43.
4. Alan Rosenthal, *Toward Majority Rule in the United States Senate.* Eagleton Institute Cases in Practical Politics, (New York: McGraw-Hill Book Company, 1962), p. 12.
5. Quoted in *Congressional Quarterly Weekly Report,* Vol. XV, No. 35 (August 30, 1957) p. 1057.
6. Quoted in Daniel M. Berman, *A Bill Becomes a Law: The Civil Rights Act of 1960,* (New York: Macmillan Company, 1962), p. 53.

7. *Ibid.*
8. H. Douglas Price, "Legislative Policy-Making," in Stephen K. Bailey (ed.), *American Politics and Government: Essays in Essentials* (New York: Basic Books, 1965), p. 102.
9. Quoted in *Revolution in Civil Rights* (Washington: Congressional Quarterly, Inc., 1965), p. 62.
10. *Ibid.*
11. *Ibid.*, pp. 44-46.
12. *Ibid.*, p. 69.

CHAPTER VII

1. See especially
   Robert K. Carr. *The House Committee on Un-American Activities, 1945-1950,* (Ithaca: Cornell University Press, 1952).
   Joseph P. Harris. *The Advice and Consent of the Senate,* (Berkeley: University of California Press, 1953).
   M. Nelson McGeary. *The Developments of Congressional Investigative Power.* (New York: Columbia University Press, 1940).
   Robert Ash Wallace. *Congressional Control of Federal Spending.* (Detroit: Wayne State University Press, 1960).
2. See Strathearn Gordon and T.G.B. Cocks, *A People's Conscience,* (London: Constable and Co., 1952).
3. Louis Smith, *American Democracy and Military Power,* quoted in Donald H. Riddle, *The Truman Committee: A Study in Congressional Responsibility* (New Brunswick: Rutgers University Press, 1964), pp. 7-8.
4. See *Congress and the Nation, 1945-1964* (Washington, D.C.: Congressional Quarterly, Inc. 1965), p. 1684.
5. Watkins v. U.S., 345 U.S. 178 (1957).
6. See Donald H. Riddle, *op. cit.*
7. William J. Keefe and Morris S. Ogul, *The American Legislative Process: Congress and the States* (Englewood Cliffs: Prentice-Hall, 1964), pp. 424-425.
8. U. S. Congress, Joint Committee on the Organization of the Congress, *Hearings on the Organization of Congress,* 89th Cong., 1st Sess., 1965.
9. U. S. Congress, Joint Committee on the Organization of the Cong ress, *op. cit.*

CHAPTER VIII

1. Commencement Address, delivered at Syracuse University, Syracuse, New York, June 6, 1965.
2. Senator William Benton. Testimony before the Douglas Subcommittee on Ethics. (U.S. Senate Committee on Labor and Public Welfare, *Hearings Before a Subcommittee to Study . . . the Establishment of a Commission on Ethics in Government),* 82nd Cong., 1st Sess., June 19-July 11, 1951, p. 45.
3. I have drawn particularly heavily upon the 1964 *Congressional Quarterly Almanac,* pp. 942-973, and upon the various relevant hearings and reports of the Senate Rules and Administration Committee which conducted the Baker investigation over a sixteen-month period, from October 1963 to March 1965.
4. See Alexander Heard, *The Costs of Democracy* (Chapel Hill: University of North Carolina Press, 1960), and Herbert Alexander, [ed.], *Studies in Money in Politics* (Princeton: Citizens' Research Foundation, 1965).
5. *New York Times,* Oct. 23, 1965, p. 63.
6. *Ibid.*
7. Alfred North Whitehead, *Symbolism: Its Meaning and Effect.* (New York: Macmillan Company, 1927), p. 88.
8. The final six paragraphs are quoted from the author's "Is Congress the Old Frontier?" in Marian D. Irish (ed.), *The Continuing Crisis in American Politics,*©1963. Prentice-Hall, Inc., Englewood Cliffs, N. J.

Bibliography

Bauer, Raymond A., Ithiel de Sola Pool, and Lewis Anthony Dexter. *American Business and Public Policy: The Politics of Foreign Trade.* New York: Atherton Press, 1963.

Berman, Daniel M. *A Bill Becomes a Law: The Civil Rights Act of 1960.* New York: Macmillan Company, 1962.*

——. *In Congress Assembled.* New York: Macmillan Company, 1964.

Bolling, Richard. *House Out of Order.* New York: E. P. Dutton and Co., 1965.

Burns, James MacGregor. *The Deadlock of Democracy: Four-Party Politics in America.* Englewood Cliffs: Prentice-Hall, 1963.*

Cater, Douglass. *Power in Washington.* New York: Random House, 1964.*

Clapp, Charles L. *The Congressman: His Work as He Sees It.* Washington, D.C.: Brookings Institution, 1963.

Clark, Joseph S. and other senators. *The Senate Establishment.* New York: Hill and Wang, 1963.*

Cleveland, James C. *We Propose: A Modern Congress.* New York: McGraw-Hill Book Co., 1966.

Congressional Quarterly, Inc. *Congress and the Nation, 1945-1964.* Washington, D.C. 1965.

——. *Congressional Quarterly Weekly Reports,* 1957-1965.

——. *Congressional Reform.* Special Report Revised, April, 1964. Washington, D.C., 1964.

——. *Revolution in Civil Rights.* Washington, D.C., 1965.

Davidson, Roger H., David M. Kovenock, and Michael O'Leary. *Congress in Crisis: Politics and Congressional Reform.* Belmont, Calif.: Wadsworth Publishing Co., 1966.

Fenno, Richard F., Jr. *The Power of the Purse: Appropriations Politics in Congress.* Boston: Little, Brown and Co., 1966.

* Available in paperback edition.

Froman, Lewis A., Jr. *The Congressional Process: Strategies, Rules, and Procedures.* Boston: Little, Brown and Co., 1967.

Getz, Robert S. *Congressional Ethics: The Conflict of Interest Issue.* Princeton: D. Van Nostrand Co., 1966.

Gross, Bertram M. *The Legislative Struggle.* New York: McGraw-Hill Book Company, 1953.

Harris, Joseph P. *The Advice and Consent of the Senate.* Berkeley: University of California Press, 1953.

Heard, Alexander. *The Costs of Democracy.* Chapel Hill: University of North Carolina Press, 1960.

Huitt, Ralph K., and Robert L. Peabody. *Congress: Two Decades of Analysis.* New York: Harper & Row, 1968-69.

Keefe, William J., and Morris S. Ogul. *The American Legislative Process: Congress and the States.* Englewood Cliffs: Prentice-Hall, 1964.

Kofmehl, Kenneth. *Professional Staffs of Congress.* Lafayette: Purdue University. Purdue Research Foundation. 1962.

Leuthold, David A. *Electioneering in a Democracy: Campaigns for Congress.* New York: John Wiley & Sons, 1968.

Lowi, Theodore J. (ed.), *Legislative Politics, U.S.A.*, 2nd ed. Boston: Little Brown and Company, 1965.*

MacNeil, Neil. *Forge of Democracy: The House of Representatives.* New York: David McKay Co., 1963.*

Mayhew, David R. *Party Loyalty Among Congressmen.* Cambridge: Harvard University Press, 1966.

Miller, Warren and Donald Stokes. *Representation in Congress.* Englewood Cliffs: Prentice-Hall, 1966.

Neustadt, Richard E. *Presidential Power, The Politics of Leadership.* New York: John Wiley & Sons, 1960.*

Polsby, Nelson W. *Congress and the Presidency.* Englewood Cliffs: Prentice-Hall, 1964.*

Riddle, Donald H. *The Truman Committee: A Study in Congressional Responsibility.* New Brunswick: Rutgers University Press, 1964.

Ripley, Randall B. *Party Leaders in the House of Representatives.* Washington, D.C.: Brookings Institution, 1967.

——. *Power in the Senate.* New York: St. Martin's Press, 1969.

Rosenthal, Alan. *Toward Majority Rule in the United States Senate.* Eagleton Institute Cases in Practical Politics. New York: McGraw-Hill Book Company, 1962.

Saloma, John S., III. *Congress and the New Politics.* Boston: Little, Brown and Co., 1969.

Scott, Andrew M., and Margaret A. Hunt. *Congress and Lobbies: Image and Reality.* Chapel Hill: University of North Carolina Press, 1966.

Truman, David B. (ed.). *The Congress and America's Future.* The American Assembly, Columbia University. Englewood Cliffs: Prentice-Hall, 1965.*

——. *The Congressional Party.* New York: John Wiley & Sons, 1959.*

Index